The A-Z of Sales Management

John Fenton is one of the leading experts on industrial selling
in the UK. After founding the Institution of Sales Engineers
in 1965 he played a major part in the formation of the
Institute of Sales Management and the Institute of Purchasing
Management. Over a number of years his experience as a
consultant and trainer has given him close involvement with
well over twenty thousand practitioners of the arts of selling
and buying. His own management role, as chairman and
managing director of the Sales Augmentation Group, a group of
companies which includes Structured Training Limited,
combines with his training and consultancy experience to make
him a unique and outstanding figure in sales and marketing
in the UK.

Also by John Fenton
in Pan Books

How to Double Your Profits Within the Year

The A-Z of
Sales Management

John Fenton

Pan Books
in association with **Heinemann**

First published 1979 by William Heinemann Ltd
This edition published 1981 by Pan Books Ltd,
Cavaye Place, London SW10 9PG
in association with William Heinemann Ltd
© John Fenton 1979
ISBN 0 330 26323 4
Printed and bound in Great Britain by
Richard Clay (The Chaucer Press) Ltd, Bungay, Suffolk

Contents

Acknowledgements 9
Preface 11

The A – Z of Industrial Salesmanship 13

Advertising and Sales Promotions 14

Blue-Assed Fly Disease 19

Company Cars 22
Credit Control 31
Customer Records 32

Decision Making 35

Exhibitions 37
Expense Accounts 40

Forecasting 44

Growth 50

Holes (Sudden) 59

If in Doubt – Ask 60
Interdepartmental Relationships 62

Job Specifications and Job Descriptions   63

Kerbside Conferences   74
Key Questions for Sales Managers   78

Leadership   80
Leadswingers   82
League Tables   82
Low-Potential Accounts   84

Memos to the Troops   90
Moonlighting   91
Motivation   92

Norms   94

Office Costs   97
Organizing Sales Conferences   97

Personal Performance   106
Post-Mortems   115
Priorities   115

Quotations and Proposals   117

Recruiting Salesmen   130
Remuneration Schemes   132

Sales Literature   136
Service Contracts   137
Strengths and Weaknesses   145
Supplier Evaluation   146

Team Spirit 150
Territories and Targets 150
Titles 151
Trade Cycles 152
Training Salesmen 155

Unwinding 156
USP 156
Utilizing Travelling Time 157

Visual Aids 160

Why Not, Why Not? 162

Xmas Presents 163

Yahoo 166

Zest 167

Postscript 168

Acknowledgements

The writing of this book has been something of a combined effort, as one aim has been for it to become the main back-up material to the sales management courses we run at Structured Training Ltd for the Institute of Sales Management.

Thanks are due to the training team of Structured Training, Peter Amis, John Morris, Jim Tappenden, David Stone, Ron Black, and Don Laurie for their contributions to the final work; again specifically to Jim Tappenden, for providing so much valuable input for the terms of employment and company car sections, and to Peter Bosworth, managing director of Sales Control and Record Systems Ltd, for his help on sales force control. And not forgetting my secretary Julie McEwan and my wife Ann, who respectively held me back from a too forthright approach to some of the seamier problems of managers today and urged me on to finishing the book almost on time and so avoiding the wrath of my very patient publisher.

Finally, grateful thanks to the companies that were willing to admit that they retained me as a consultant and have allowed me to use some examples of what I did for them to illustrate this book.

Preface

At least half the sales managers fortunate enough to be reading this are still salesmen at heart; thinking like salesmen: still trying to be accepted as 'one of the boys' rather than as leaders of men.

They gained their promotion because they were the best salesmen in the company, and able to get on well with the people around them. But because they are still salesmen at heart, they are reluctant to change things they know need changing; to implement effective reporting, planning, and control systems; to introduce more practical ways of motivating and paying the salesmen; to throw out procedures that have been allowed to continue unaltered since before they themselves joined the company.

They worry constantly about the risk of annoying their salesmen too much and making the situation worse, rather than better. Consequently, they do little but perpetuate the general aura of passive indifference which the company has probably generated for more years than its employees can remember.

This book shows a sales manager how to be different. How to succeed where others failed. How to get the best out of his salesmen, be in complete control of his sales operation, and still have his salesmen's respect and friendship.

The book is essentially about people – how to treat, motivate, and lead them to victory against all odds – internal and external.

It is written to separate the wood from the trees and provide guidance on the bare essentials of the task of managing an industrial sales operation – the top priorities of the job.

It shows how to achieve consistent results and how to build a team of salesmen who themselves strive for continual improvement of personal performance. And it shows how the sales manager keeps his cool while all this is happening.

When these priorities have been mastered and fully implemented, the rest will be easy – all the way to the top.

John Fenton

Works Notices by Kenneth Aitken

The A–Z of Industrial Salesmanship

It's not every author who gets the chance to put in a legitimate plug for another of his books, so early. But in this case, it's *very* legitimate.

You won't ever succeed as a sales manager unless you really know – in depth – what your salesmen should be doing. You don't have to be a better salesman than your salesmen; you *do* need to know in detail how their job must be done; what they have to do to get the required results with the minimum of wasted effort.

The chances are, you have spent quite a few years as a salesman before promotion came your way. Don't fall into the trap of thinking you know all there is to know about selling, based on the strength of your own experience. Think back to the days when *you* were learning how to sell. Who taught you? What kind of training did you get? How much of what you know was picked up off the seat of your pants, out there in the field, or by following the bad habits of other salesmen?

So how do you know that what you've been doing all these years is the *best* way; or the most *economical* way; or the most *effective* way?

Read my first book, *The A–Z of Industrial Salesmanship*. Use it to form the basis of the standards of performance for your own sales force. Use it in conjunction with this book. Together, the two books will bring you success, just as the methods, techniques, and principles they contain have brought *me* success.

Advertising and Sales Promotion

Don't ever lose sight of the main objective for your advertising and sales promotion activity – which is to generate inquiries for your sales force to follow up subsequently.

Why advertise at all? Why not leave things completely to the sales force? A recent survey of about 1,100 British companies gives the answer.

Size of company	Average number of persons who influence buying decisions	Average number of persons visited by salesmen
Less than 200 employees	3.43	1.72
200–400 employees	4.85	1.75
401–1,000 employees	5.81	1.90
More than 1,000 employees	6.50	1.65

So how else do you get to all those decision influencers whom your salesmen are missing? Plus any potential customers you didn't hitherto know existed, of course.

Designing Advertisements

Your advertisements and mailing shots should always follow the AIDA format:

ATTENTION (picture or simple headline)
INTEREST (carrot – preferably about money)
DESIRE (what *could* be in it for him)
ACTION (fill in the coupon or pick up the phone)

Use pictures with life in them, not 'still-life' shots of the equipment, grossly overtouched, highlighted and air-brushed. *Never* use drawings or sketches of the products; all you are saying to the reader is – 'we haven't actually made one yet'.

Feature customers or your own people in your advertisements. Those customers will be with you for life. Try to make your picture identify with the reader, or vice versa, so that whatever the people in the picture are doing, the reader feels like doing too.

Or try a format which gets the reader *doing* something. The advertisement shown in figure 1 consistently pulls in over forty inquiries each time it is used, in a medium circulation journal which goes to the same people every month. Reasonable proof also that to get consistent results from advertising you need to advertise consistently.

Don't cram too much into too small a space. Blank white space is as powerful in an advertisement as silence is in a selling situation.

Use bookmarks rather than page advertisements in any publication which has a long life as a work of reference. Or the outside front or back cover or spine of the book.

One of the best positions to place an advertisement in the average technical or trade journal is on the left-hand page facing the journal's reader inquiry card. Everyone who wants details of anything advertised in that journal will turn to the reader card to send for further information. While they are filling in the card, they must see your advertisement. So they could well circle *your* number as well. Mission accomplished.

Which Media to Use

Don't guess. Get all the readership breakdown details from a selection of journals and calculate the *true* cost per valid reader.

Say you want to get your advertisement in front of production managers. A certain magazine has a circulation of 20,000, but its readership breakdown indicates that only 10,000 copies go to production managers. Cost of a whole page advertisement is, say, £500. Thus, true cost per valid reader is

$$\frac{£500}{10,000} = 5p.$$

Compare *all* the media you are considering on this basis, unless there are other valid criteria to make you choose differently.

A copy of *British Rate and Data*, published monthly by

1 Do you provide your salesmen with a standardized method for keeping customer records?

2 Do your salesmen keep their customer records up to date — and *USE* them?

3 Do you make sure a salesman who leaves the company doesn't take his customer records with him?

4 Do you know how much prospecting work your salesmen need to do to achieve the company's 'new business' target?

5 If you can answer "Yes" to question 4, do you know if your salesmen are actually *doing* the amount of prospecting work required?

6 Do you receive a detailed plan from your salesmen of where they will be next week?

7 Are more than 40% of your salesmen's calls 'by appointment'?

8 Do you know how much business your salesmen are chasing that your company has quoted for?

9 Do you know how much of this business is likely to result in firm orders NEXT MONTH?

10 Do your salesmen prepare for you a forecast of how much business they reckon they will produce for the company during the next period?

11 Is this forecast in a sufficiently detailed form so that you can pinpoint any specific customer that isn't coming up to

sufficiently legible, detailed and accurate for the company to produce a quotation and be certain it will fulfil the customer's requirements?

13 Do your salesmen submit a weekly report of the customers they have called upon — and what happened?

14 If the answer to question 13 is 'Yes', does anyone use the information on the weekly reports, rather than just file them away after a general check?

15 Do you know if any salesmen are neglecting part of your product range?

16 Do you know your company's average order value?

17 Do you know your company's 'calls to quotations' ratio?

18 Do you know your company's 'quotations to orders' ratio?

Totals

As a manager, all your answers should be YES.

Get a NO more than half a dozen times and you should be starting to worry about exactly how much business your inefficiency is losing the company.

After that comes the 'but what the hell do I do about it with the time I've got available' stage, and that's where we come in.

We have the solution, and it isn't time-consuming.

If you would like us to provide a solution to your problems why not contact us?

Sales Control & Record Systems Ltd

Concorde House, 24 Warwick New Road, Royal Leamington Spa, CV32 5JH Telephone: 0926 37621-4

Figure 1. Example of an advertisement which uses the AIDA format.

Maclean Hunter Ltd, London, will give you all the basic information you need.

Writing Editorials

You need to develop the ability to write good editorial copy for trade and technical magazines. A good article is worth umpteen pages of advertisements. Six good articles about six good customers who have benefited significantly from using your products, when reprinted, give you the contents of a new addition to your range of sales literature – and something much more powerful than your usual brochures.

A good editorial story should be slanted towards the *application* of your products by one or more customers. The article should be 80 per cent about the customer and 20 per cent about the application and your products. Do it the other way round and no editor will touch the story. Neither would it do *you* any good if he did.

Don't Forget

Always keep your salesmen fully informed about what advertisements and articles are scheduled for publication, and in which media. Give each salesman advance copies and lots of reprints to hand out to customers and prospective customers.

Blue-Assed Fly Disease

Do you love working in a panic situation ?

Many managers do. Maybe it's a question of adrenalin flow. Everything is left to the last minute. Everyone in the department has to work overtime. The deadline is met, but only after everyone's lost a couple of pounds in sweat.

Only the manager who suffers from BAF disease gets any kind of feeling of satisfaction for a job well done, if the job has been done that way. His staff reckon he's a pain. Inconsiderate and irresponsible. And when you get down to brass tacks, it only happens because of a lack of self-discipline, leading to a lack of planning.

Remember the old office joke, hanging on the wall . . .

If you can keep your head while everyone
round you is losing theirs – it means you
haven't the slightest idea what's going on.

Well, the good manager works to the opposite of this. He keeps his head *and* knows the score. He sets an example and calms everyone down.

He has learned the secret of planning. Start at the point in time when the job has to be completed – and work *back* towards now. Not the other way round. From the time plan, establish what has to be done, who has to do it, and delegate each task clearly, building in deadlines for each delegated action. Then relax and have it all happen, being available to mop up any hang-ups or unforeseen problems.

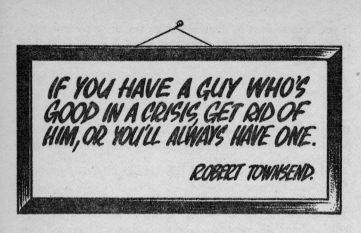

IF YOU HAVE A GUY WHO'S GOOD IN A CRISIS, GET RID OF HIM, OR YOU'LL ALWAYS HAVE ONE.

ROBERT TOWNSEND.

Using Your Time More Profitably

A number of business surveys have indicated that the average sales manager works fifty to sixty hours a week. He takes work home with him and lives with a wife who struggles, often unsuccessfully, to keep him human.

He carries his work, often unfinished, back to the office. There he will have one hour alone each day, being interrupted every eight minutes by subordinates or other executives seeking advice or answers to problems. Most of these problems are things other employees are being paid to resolve.

He spends 80 per cent of his time communicating and only 20 per cent doing creative work.

The Chest and Heart Association say this is fatal.

So set yourself some objectives:

1 To reduce interruptions by 50 per cent.
2 To reduce time spent on the telephone by 50 per cent.
3 To reduce time spent on correspondence by 30 per cent.
4 To double the time spent on planning and thinking.
5 To allow half an hour every day for self-analysis and creativity.
6 To delegate properly a further 20 per cent of your own workload.
7 To make full use of your secretary.

If you need to start by analysing what you do at present, get your secretary to list everything that happens for a full week. It will frighten you to death.

Costings

If your working year contains 238 days, your salary is £10,000 p.a. and the company's overheads are 200 per cent, your time is costing this:

1 minute	£ 0.30
5 minutes	£ 1.50
10 minutes	£ 3.00
30 minutes	£ 9.00
1 hour	£ 18.00
1 day	£126.00

This doesn't include your car and expenses.

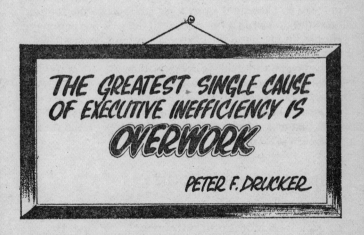

THE GREATEST SINGLE CAUSE OF EXECUTIVE INEFFICIENCY IS OVERWORK

PETER F. DRUCKER

Company Cars

Most British industrial companies provide their salesmen and sales managers with a car, and pay all reasonable, properly incurred business expenses for running the car. Some, on the other hand, require their sales staff to provide their own car, and pay a depreciation and running allowance, plus petrol and oil costs incurred on business. I'll deal with this latter method at the end of this section.

The sales manager cannot ever afford to allow any salesman to abuse in any way the privileges attaching to the company car. Stick to the laid down rules at all times. If one person gets an edge, like being allowed to tow a trailer, or being allowed to take the car abroad for his holidays, or fits a quadraphonic stereo system with built-in speakers, then the rest of the sales force will expect similar treatment. The sales manager who allows these things will therefore need to budget for the cost over the whole of the sales force car fleet, or consider any reduction in residual value which might apply when the cars are traded in for new ones.

Car User's Handbook

The company should provide every user of a company car with an explicit set of instructions covering the car's use. Here is a sample set.

Rules for the Use of Company Cars

1 Driving Licences and Authority to Drive Company Cars

(a) The person must be in possession of a current driving licence and have the company's authority to drive one of its vehicles, which authority must be given by the company secretary.

(b) The person's driving licence must have been produced for scrutiny by the company secretary, or in his absence, a director.

If at any time the driver's licence is endorsed or he is disqualified from driving, the company secretary must be informed immediately.

It is the responsibility of the driver of the vehicle to see that it is not driven by anyone other than authorized company employees. Special written permission must be obtained from the company secretary for the car to be used by any other driver not falling into this category.

2 Acceptance of Vehicle and Company Rules

At the time of taking over a company car, the company secretary will ask the driver to inspect the vehicle and agree its condition and to sign a form of receipt which will incorporate any existing faults, etc. Additionally all drivers will be asked to sign for a copy of the company's rules for the use of company cars and their signature will be taken as their acceptance of these rules.

If permission is given for a person other than the authorized driver to use the car, in addition to inspecting the person's driving licence, the company secretary must have a signature from that person acknowledging receipt of the company's rules for the use of company cars.

3 Fixtures, Fittings and Modifications

No fixtures such as aerials, roof racks, towing apparatus, stickers may be attached to company vehicles without prior written permission from the company secretary. When handing vehicles back to the company such attachments must remain unless adequate rectification work is carried out professionally to restore the vehicle to its former condition.

No change or alterations may be made to the mechanical or structural specification as delivered of any company vehicle.

4 Warranty

When a new car is handed to a driver a copy of the manufacturer's warranty is also given to the driver. It is the driver's responsibility to ensure that any costs which may rise and which fall under the terms of the warranty are reported to the company secretary *in advance* of any work being carried out and if the driver cannot obtain free of charge repairs from a garage licensed by the manufacturer, no charges may be incurred without prior written permission from the company secretary. If any charges are incurred without following this rule they must be borne by the driver since the manufacturer will not accept responsibility for work already carried out.

5 Cleaning and Maintenance

When a company car has been allocated to a particular driver it is that person's responsibility to keep the car clean and to ensure that the vehicle is regularly serviced in accordance with the requirements laid down by the manufacturers and specified in the maintenance book of the particular model of car.

Unless contrary arrangements exist in writing between the company and the driver, the company will reimburse the driver for amounts spent on regular servicing provided a receipt is submitted to the company accompanied by a claim for reimbursement detailed on a company expense voucher.

Any other maintenance or repair work or replacement of parts including tyres must be approved in advance by the company and reimbursement will only be made against production of an authorization. Full details of the work required and the cost involved must be given.

6 Fuel, etc.

In addition to keeping the vehicle regularly serviced, it is the driver's responsibility to see that the oil level, water level, topping up of the battery, brake fluid, clutch fluid, and tyre pressures are kept constantly in the correct state. Petrol octane ratings, oil grades, and all other fluids used must conform to manufacturer's recommendations as laid down in the driver's handbook.

Unless contrary arrangements exist in writing between the company and the driver, the company will only reimburse the driver for petrol and oil used on company business. Claims must be submitted on an expense voucher signed by the individual and accompanied by receipted bills. All bills should be listed and a deduction shown for that part of the fuel attributable to private mileage.

7 Garaging
No car whether belonging to the company or privately owned may be parked on the company's premises without prior consent. Any costs incurred by drivers for garaging cars must be the driver's responsibility.

8 Fines
The company cannot, under any circumstances, accept responsibility for parking or other fines incurred by drivers.

9 Insurance
(a) General A general motor vehicle insurance is expensive and annually getting more so. All vehicles used within the company are insured on a fleet basis which enables the company to enjoy a larger no-claim bonus than would be possible by insuring individual vehicles. This means, however, that the accident record is calculated on a fleet aggregate, and it is incumbent upon every driver to exercise special care in respect of the vehicle within his control, otherwise he will incur expense which will affect the premium rating for all the cars used by the company.

(b) Premium To keep the premium within reasonable limits we have agreed with our insurers to accept a proportion of the costs of each claim. Provided our driver is in no way to blame for the accident and the identity of the other party or parties involved is known, it is sometimes possible to recover some or all of this excess. It is emphasized, however, that any accident in which a company car is involved will probably cost us a considerable amount of money at the time the repairs are carried out, and will also jeopardize our chances of avoiding an increase in premium when the insurance is due for renewal.

(c) Damage or Injury The driver of any vehicle which is involved in an accident which causes damage or injury to any person, vehicle or animal is required to give his name and address, the name and address of the owner and the registration number of the vehicle and the name of his insurance company to any person having reasonable grounds for requiring such information. IT IS IMPORTANT THAT HE GIVES NO FURTHER INFOR-

MATION. If for some reason is is not possible to give this information at the time of the accident, the matter must be reported to the police as soon as possible AND WITHIN TWENTY-FOUR HOURS OF THE OCCURRENCE.

In addition, in the case of an accident involving injury to another person or to animals, the driver is responsible for notifying the police of the occurrence and must produce his insurance certificate to the police constable attending the accident or any other person having reasonable grounds for seeing it. The accident must be reported to a police station or to a police constable within twenty-four hours. If the driver is not then able to produce the certificate he must in any event produce it in person within five days after the accident to such police station as he may specify at the time of reporting the accident in the first place.

For security reasons insurance certificates are kept by the company secretary. A fascimile of the certificate of insurance is provided with each vehicle however, and this will be renewed annually in early April. All drivers should make sure that it is with the vehicle at all times. Replacement copies can be obtained from the company secretary's office if necessary.

(d) **Loss**   In the case of loss of a company vehicle, the police and the company secretary must be immediately informed. Full details of the contents of the car must also be given to the company secretary. If any contents are stolen from a company car the police and the company secretary should be immediately notified.

Drivers should note particularly that only company property is insured by the company and they should make their own arrangements to cover personal effects.

All company cars should be kept locked when not in use and contents should be stored out of sight, preferably in the boot. If a car is stolen the company is required to prove to the insurance company that there has been no negligence and therefore the company must hold the driver responsible in the event of negligence.

(e) **Claims**   It is a condition of the insurance policy that the insurers are notified of *all* accidents even if apparently of no consequence. The driver must, therefore, as soon as possible after the accident get from the company secretary an accident report form which must be completed and returned to the company secretary's office within twenty-four hours. All the information required on the form must be completed, and if necessary, the company secretary's office will give every assistance in its completion, but in any event the driver should note that whenever possible the following particulars should appear in the form:

(i) The name and address of the third party driver and the name and address of his insurers.

(ii) The names and addresses of all passengers in both the company car and the third party's vehicle.

(iii) Names and addresses of all witnesses. It will be of considerable assistance if statements can be obtained from all witnesses at the time of the accident.

Experience shows that if these are not obtained at the time, their value is usually negligible after any interval of time.

(iv) Particulars of the police attending, i.e. name, number and division.

A detailed sketch must be provided showing the relative position of the vehicle before and after the accident together with details of the roads in the vicinity, e.g. whether they are major or minor roads and as many relevant measurements as possible.

If the vehicle belonging to the company is undrivable, the driver is responsible for making adequate arrangements for the vehicle to be towed to a garage and the name and address of the garage where the vehicle can be inspected must be stated on the claim form.

UNDER NO CIRCUMSTANCES MAY REPAIRS BE PUT IN HAND UNTIL THE INSURANCE COMPANY HAS GIVEN ITS AGREEMENT.

The company secretary will give the necessary authority.

An estimate of the repairs required to be carried out showing details and cost of both labour and materials must be obtained and sent to the company secretary's office as soon as possible.

A driver should not UNDER ANY CIRCUMSTANCES express any opinion one way or another on the degree of responsibility for the accident. Just exchange the particulars mentioned in 9(c) and nothing more.

Please note also that no statements should be made to the police without written permission from the company secretary. This is particularly important in cases involving death or injury and leading to an inquest or inquiry, as the driver will have to be legally represented and would not wish to prejudice his position in any way.

10 Seat Belts
Seat belts are fitted to all company cars. Drivers and front seat passengers should wear them on *all* journeys.

11 Road Fund Licence
The road fund licence for each vehicle will automatically be renewed when due, but in the event that the new licence is not received by the driver within fourteen days of the expiry date, the company secretary should be immediately notified by telephone.

12 Travel Overseas
No company vehicle may be taken out of the country without written permission from the company secretary or managing director of the company.

The company's insurance policy covers the use of the vehicles in Great Britain, Northern Ireland, the Isle of Man and the Channel Islands. Before travelling with the vehicle anywhere else, the driver, having first obtained permission, must inform the company secretary at least seven days beforehand, giving a list of the countries to be visited and the relevant dates. A green insurance certificate will then be issued which must accompany the vehicle. On return to England this certificate should be returned to the company secretary for cancellation.

Unless the journey is on approved company business, the cost of the green insurance certificate will be charged to the driver and must be paid before the journey commences.

13 General Security
At all times when leaving the vehicle unattended, the driver must ensure that all windows are closed, the ignition key removed and the vehicle securely locked.

14 Personal Baggage
Articles of any kind carried in the vehicle and not the property of the company are at the risk of the owner of the property and the company accepts no responsibility for such property.

15 Permitted Use
Subject to the restrictions already stipulated, private vehicles may only be used for social, domestic and pleasure purposes and used for the business of the company, excluding the carriage of

passengers for hire or reward. Company vehicles may not be used for any type of motoring sport, including racing, rallying or pace making, whether on the public highway or on private land.

Commercial vehicles may only be used in connection with the company's business.

16 Priority Use

The company reserves the right to take back any car at any time should an occasion arise where the company has an imperative need for the vehicle.

Car Size and Status

'Never fall in love with the company car' is the suggestion I make in my first book, yet still many salesmen and sales executives fall into this emotional trap and wind up in trouble.

More people see status as a larger car than any other single item they own or have the use of. Many companies reward consistent performance by giving that person a slightly better car than his colleagues, but this only acts as a motivating factor if the companies are also prepared to give the person back his smaller car if he *stops* performing.

· It is a sound system and, with 42 per cent of the 1976–7 sales fleet car business, a major reason why Ford introduced nine models of the Cortina, from the basic saloon to the Ghia Estate, and three engine sizes. Twenty-seven variations of one model – enough for even the most complex hierarchy of salesmen.

If a sales manager has any say in the matter, he shouldn't allow the size of car given to the company accountant or the works manager to have any influence on the most *suitable* car for the sales force. The average annual mileage for an industrial salesman in 1976 was 28,000 miles. The average for sales managers was 32,000 miles. Comfort, safety, and freedom from fatigue are key factors in a salesman's consistent performance.

HOW TO SPOT A COMPANY CAR

1. They travel faster in ALL gears, especially reverse.

2. They accelerate at a phenomenal rate.

3. They enjoy a much shorter braking distance.

4. They have a much tighter turning circle.

5. They can take ramps at twice the speed of private cars.

6. Battery, water, oil and tyre pressures are not needed to be checked nearly so often.

7. The floor is shaped just like an ashtray.

8. They burn only the petrol with the highest Green Shield stamp rate.

9. They do not require to be garaged at night.

10. Can be driven for up to 100 miles with the oil warning light flashing.

11. They need cleaning less often.

12. The suspension is reinforced to allow carriage of concrete slabs and other heavy building materials.

13. They are adapted to allow reverse gear to be engaged while the car is still moving forwards.

14. The tyre walls are designed to allow bumping into and over kerbstones.

15. Unusual and alarming engine noises are easily eliminated by the adjustment of the fitted radio volume control.

16. No security needed. May be left anywhere, unlocked, with the keys in the ignition.

Credit Cards

A good way to minimize business holdups due to car break-downs is for the company to allocate its sales force Avis or Hertz credit cards. These enable the salesman to hire a car at a local depot without delays, the charges being billed direct to the company.

The Salesman's Own Car

Most people look after things that belong to them better than they look after other people's property. They also normally get greater satisfaction from driving a car they have chosen themselves. There are no restrictions on the use of the car to annoy its owner or his wife.

There is a slightly increasing trend towards encouraging salesmen to buy their own cars. Most companies operating this way help by offering interest-free loans, but condition these loans by specifying size limits for the car and maximum life before it should be renewed. The owner then receives a depreciation and maintenance allowance and is reimbursed for business petrol and oil or receives an additional mileage allowance to cover petrol and oil.

Don't ask me for guideline allowance figures. They change almost every month, and the best places to get this information from are the headquarters of the AA or the RAC. Both produce regular surveys of car running costs.

Credit Control

Don't ever let the accounts department chase your customers for payment without first checking with you or someone senior in your sales office to make sure there are no good reasons for the delay in payment.

Personally, I believe it is up to the salesman to secure payment of overdue accounts. After all, he took the order, and he should have checked out the customer for credit worthiness and established the ground-rules for payment at the order–acceptance stage.

Okay, I know life isn't always like that. But try to get as near the optimum as you can.

If your company is blessed with its own computer, there is one little gimmick you might find useful as well as effective in securing payment without more ado.

Get the *computer* to write the customer a letter – as a printout. Like this:

I am the Bloggs Pumps Computer.

As yet, no one but me knows that there is a balance outstanding on your July account.

If, however, I have not processed a payment from you within fourteen days, I am programmed to tell the office manager, who will then deal with the matter. Why should we involve him?

Customer Records

Always provide your salesmen with a standard system of customer records, one which is easy to use and easy to keep up to date.

If your salesmen spend the majority of their time selling on a repeat business basis, provide them with customer record files, foolscap size, not cards. Then all the assorted paperwork they need to keep on each customer can be stored in one place, in the customer record file, and the sides of the file itself become the call record. Figure 2 shows a typical customer record file from the SCRS system.

A good filing system for customer record cards or files works on a 'date of next call' basis, not alphabetically. Thus, after a call, the salesman fills in the details on his card or file, plus the date and objective of the *next* call, which he has agreed with the

Company	Address				Tele	Code
Type of Business		Contact	Position	BestDay/Time		
		1				
		2				
Turnover	Number of Employees	4				
		5				
Products used	Competition	6				
		7				
		8				
		9				

Call Record							
Date of Call	Con−tacts	What Happened	Order Value	Aim of Next Call	Date	Business Lost	
						WhoTo	Reason

Figure 2. Example of a customer record file.

customer before departing. The record is filed back into the salesman's system in the month during which the next call is due. So at the end, of, say, May, every customer due for a call during June is already filed under June. No time consuming sorting through the records every week to establish who's due for a call. Result – happier salesmen.

If a salesman leaves, make sure you get all his records back. Everything is legally company property anyway, even any cards or books he may have purchased himself. All these records, if properly maintained, are essential to the salesman who replaces the man leaving. They can reduce his initial time up to full effectiveness by six months – and you know how much money that will save, and how much extra business it will produce.

D

Decision Making

Most managers are lousy decision makers.

Maybe it's that feeling of insecurity generated by the chairman. Or maybe it's just that making a decision on something when you've run out of time before all the facts have been collected gives you a feeling that risking being wrong is going to come back on you and everyone else is going to escape scot-free.

There used to be a simple rule on decision making in the businessman's rule book: *any decision is better than none at all.* This rule is still true today. Decisions made that are subsequently found to be wrong can be changed, and changed fast.

But there are a few more rules that can reduce the chances of being wrong:

Decisions about Solving Problems

1 Define the problem. A problem correctly defined is a problem 80 per cent solved.
2 Pinpoint the causes of the problem. You cannot find a solution until you are sure about the causes.
3 Establish the possible solutions.
4 Decide the best solution. Selected from all possible solutions.
5 Implement the best solution. Fast and firmly.

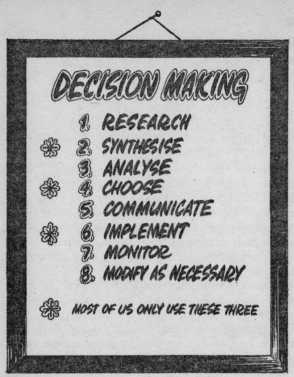

DECISION MAKING

1. RESEARCH
* 2. SYNTHESISE
3. ANALYSE
* 4. CHOOSE
5. COMMUNICATE
* 6. IMPLEMENT
7. MONITOR
8. MODIFY AS NECESSARY

* MOST OF US ONLY USE THESE THREE

Decisions on People Problems

1 Get all the facts. Get both sides of the story. Talk to everyone involved. Check back on the records. Gauge opinions, attitudes and feelings.

2 Don't jump to conclusions. Don't allow your own personal feelings to interfere. Fit all the facts together and make sure the complete jigsaw puzzle makes logical sense.

3 Consider all the possible actions. Check company policies. Consult other executives if you feel this necessary. Consider the effect of your action on the individual, your team, and the rest of the company. Don't panic and chicken out, if you still think you're right.

4 Take action. And don't ever pass the buck to someone else.

5 Check the results of the action. Did you achieve your objective?

Exhibitions

If you get landed with the task of organizing your company's stand at a trade exhibition, you'll find it one of the most time-consuming and nerve-racking jobs you've ever had. There are about sixty separate events that go into the planning of a trade stand, from conception or decision to exhibit, to opening day.

Done properly, the organizing takes a year. Yet most companies only start getting down to it about three months before the exhibition itself.

One way to start is to hire two films from Video Arts Ltd, Dumbarton House, 68 Oxford Street, London WIN 9LA (01-637 7288), and show them to everyone involved in the planning team. These films are entitled *It'll be Okay on the Day* and *How not to Exhibit Yourself*. Better still, attend one of Structured Training's *Planning and Manning an Exhibition Stand* workshops held at the Metropole Hotel, National Exhibition Centre, Birmingham, and the Bowater Conference Centre, Knightsbridge, London, once or twice each year.

Planning an exhibition stand entails using a process called project management. It is different and separate from the day-to-day disciplines in the company.

A project like an exhibition stand has deadline urgency. It has a beginning, a middle and an end. The end is the date by which the project has to be completed.

A project is superimposed on other work, and is handled by people who have their regular responsibilities to discharge as well.

A project runs across departmental boundaries, needing to harness people with a variety of skills, scattered through different departments.

A project is a pioneering enterprise. There is a much greater probability of unforeseen problems.

The Video Arts film *It'll be Okay on the Day* lists the top ten rules of project management. I cannot do better than to give you this list unabridged, with their kind permission.

The Top Ten Rules of Project Management

1 *Agree objectives*: the objectives must be established at the first meeting, and agreed by everyone present.

2 *Establish command*: the man in charge must be accepted as carrying the full authority necessary to bring the project to a successful conclusion.

3 *Establish responsibilities*: the separate responsibilities for sections or stages of the project must be clearly defined and each one firmly allocated to a single manager.

4 *Plan all dates backwards from D-Day*: a detailed project planning chart must be drawn up, with the dates worked out to give sufficient time to avoid the last-minute panic. The chart and dates must be circulated to all those responsible.

5 *Every manager must have his own calendar*: as well as the overall project chart, each responsible manager must have his own calendar of his key dates.

6 *Fix key meetings a long way in advance*: there will not be many key meetings which all the project team managers have to attend, but they are likely to be almost impossible to fix at short notice. It is no bad thing to fix them all at the first meeting, together with agreement on what actions must be completed and what information obtained in time for each.

7 *Circulate information religiously*: this includes, in particular, minutes of all meetings – details of each person's responsibilities; details of all action decisions; information on any changes in the project programme; and the complete project chart as soon as it is complete and whenever it is revised.

8 *Chase progress relentlessly*: especially when the project is superimposed on other work, constant reminding is essential. The project leader's secretary will probably need a separate desk diary to enter up the successive completion dates for chasing.

9 *Check budget regularly*: the project leader must get each man-

SMT-PULLMAX
MACH'76 Enquiry

Products of interest

Notes on specific details	Metal Cutting	Metal Forming
General Information	☐ ST 10-220	☐ P31-CNC220
Budget Price	☐ ST 14-220	☐ Pullmax Universal
Quotation	☐ ST 20-220	☐ Pullmax Beveller X91
Time Studies	☐ VHF/3/3U/3UBS	☐ Pullmax Ring Roller 731
Demonstration	☐ Unidrill 1000	☐ Kumla Rolls PV7H
		☐ Ursviken Press Brakes
		☐ Ursviken Guillotine
		☐ Wikstroms BW300
		☐ Wikstroms BW225/4DV

Literature taken at MACH'76 stand

☐ General Catalogue m/c   ☐ General Catalogue m/f

Reason for interest

☐ Expanding production   OTHERS

☐ Replacing existing plant

☐ Seeking to reduce labour force

Name_____ Position_____

Company_____

Address_____

Telephone Number_____ Extension_____

Best Time For Sales Engineer To Call_____

Figure 3.

ager to let him have a detailed breakdown of his budget as soon as possible, and regularly compare committed expenditure with the budget figure, issuing red alerts immediately he sees a hint of overspending.

10 *Resist alterations ruthlessly*: a few alterations may be inevitable, and some more may be too important to exclude; but remember that it is alterations after the programme is agreed that constitute the greatest single hazard to the enterprise. So it is worth taking a lot of trouble to ensure that everyone who might contribute or be affected has been consulted and had a chance to have his say before you lock off the programme.

D-Day

When the day of the exhibition finally arrives, there are at least three critical things to have considered:

1 That you have a stand manager who has been delegated complete authority, even over the chairman.
2 That you have a stand manning rota that provides for a maximum of two-hour-long shifts (that's all the guards outside Buckingham Palace do).
3 That you have a proper system for logging inquiries.

Figure 3 shows an exhibition enquiry form that I designed for a stand at the 1976 Machine Tool Exhibition. The pad of forms went inside a standard A4 survey pad and, just in case a stand salesman was surprised by a prospective customer at a time he was not carrying his survey pad (sacrilege indeed) we also produced a miniature version for his jacket pocket. This particular exhibitor logged more than 1,200 inquiries during the 1976 show, using this system.

Expense Accounts

If you operate a lunch or subsistence allowance, make sure you keep up with the current costs of pub lunches, two-star accommodation, *table d'hote* dinners, etc. If your allowances are out of phase with the going rates, you'll demotivate your salesmen and encourage them to cook the books on their expense claims.

It is a measure of the attitudes that exist within some sales forces that even when the company states clearly that a lunch allowance is intended to cover only the *difference* between a lunch taken outside and one taken in the works canteen (for which all workers have to pay), this still seems to be a constant cause of demotivation and complaints that the allowance is too low.

Make sure the expenses claim form used by your salesman is designed to give you the kind of detailed information for which you need to look. Also get the claim form to separate out VAT. You'll be your company accountant's friend for life.

Figure 4 shows an example of a well-designed monthly expenses claim form.

Name _____

DAY	DATE	JOURNEY	PETROL & OIL		REPAIRS		HOTELS		MEALS		FARE
			£	p	£	p	£	p	£	p	£
MON											
TUES											
WED											
THUR											
FRI											
MON											
TUES											
WED											
THUR											
FRI											
MON											
TUES											
WED											
THUR											
FRI											
MON											
TUES											
WED											
THUR											
FRI											
MON											
TUES											
WED											
THUR											
FRI											
		TOTALS									
		Less Private Petrol									
		TOTAL Business Petrol									
H.Q. USE ONLY		Less V.A.T									
		TAX EXCLUSIVE VALUES									

Figure 4. Example of a monthly expenses claim form.

Date _____

PHONE		CUSTOMER ENTERTAINMENT			OTHER EXPENSES			GRAND TOTAL	
£	p	Name of Customer	£	p	Details	£	p	£	p
						Less Private Petrol			
						TOTAL CLAIMED			

Forecasting

Your company's sales forecast for next year, or whatever the next selling period may be, has to be put together mainly by your sales force, because it is the sales force that has to be committed to the task of *achieving* the forecast sales.

You'll never really commit a salesman to achieving any objective if he hasn't been involved in deciding what the objective should be, and why.

It takes three months for any salesman to produce a meaningful forecast of the business his territory should produce next year. Not three months' solid work, of course, three months during which the salesman is making his normal calls, but at the same time, asking an additional question or two of everyone he meets:

I've got to produce a forecast of what business will come from my territory next year. Could you give me any idea of what your requirements are likely to be between January and December?

And so on: think of the commitment they get from the customers for next year, on this basis.

Don't expect an accurate forecast if you give your salesmen a week in which to prepare it. All you'll get is an overall guess based on last year. Totally useless.

Use a form for sales forecasting like the one shown in figure 5. Get your salesmen to complete as many forms as they can over that three month period. Get them also to list business in order of potential – biggest first, smallest last.

You'll see that the form provides for breaking down each

individual customer or prospect forecast into quarterly periods and according to the products involved. There is also a column for noting the minimum calls the salesman reckons he needs to allocate to each customer next year – another thing he could agree with the customer when asking those forecasting questions.

Having the 'minimum calls' column next to the 'total forecast' column wasn't just an accident. You know how many calls each of your salesmen are likely to be able to make during next year. So count up the calls allocated in the 'minimum calls' column, from the top of the first sheet, until you arrive at the total calls possible in the year. Draw a line across the forecast sheet at that point. Then add up the business in the 'total forecast' column from the top of sheet one until you get to the line. That's the total amount of business this salesman has got time to get, if you accept his minimum call figures.

You now have a superb starting point from which to decide, by agreement, the salesman's final sales target for next year. Bring in his personal performance ratios which are detailed in the section entitled 'personal performance' and you have everything you need to get the very best out of every salesman.

Total Forecast

When you have established the sales target for each salesman, if these targets are still in the same format as the original forecasts, which they should be, you can total them all up on a card like the one shown in figure 6 and produce a total company forecast which should keep production, finance and everyone else happy. As long as you achieve it, of course.

This system of forecasting doesn't suit *every* type of business, only *most* kinds, but the principles can be used, even in cases where 90 per cent of your business is 'contract' or 'one-offs'.

LIST CUSTOMERS IN ORDER OF POTENTIAL, GREATEST FIRST **SALES FORECAST** for year 1980 Salesman **J. WATSON**

Sheet 1 of 4 Sheets

CUSTOMER	INDUSTRY CATEGORY	MINIMUM CALLS NEEDED IN YEAR	TOTAL FORECAST	FORECAST SPREAD				PRODUCT GROUP BREAKDOWN									
				FIRST QUARTER	SECOND QUARTER	THIRD QUARTER	FOURTH QUARTER	0	1	2	3	4	5	6	7	8	9
TOTALS BROUGHT FORWARD																	
EATON E Co	C	20	2400	600	600	600	600		1600	600							
BIRDESMILL	A	20	2200	600	600	500	600					1000		600			600
BRT	C	20	2000	600	400	500	500		2000							
V BLAND	B	20	1600	600	600	500	500	1000					600			
PAYSON E Co	H	20	1500	500		500	500			1600						
W. WALTON	A	10	1300	500		500	500		400	950	500					
CK VALVES	D	20	1300	400	1300	300	300		400					500		
A. RICHARDS	D	6	1200	400			400			1200						
GIS TUBES	D	20	1000	500	200	200	200		300	300			505	500	052	
TOBIN & Co	C	6	1000	400	100	200	600					050	200	200		
BERRY BROS	F	10	950	320	050	250	450						059			
A. McGINTY	D	10	950	320	200	190	340				450	059				054
POTBERRY & G	G	9	900	300	200		200	300	300							
BREEDON SMITH	A	9	900	340	100		340					450	450			
ASH E Co	A	9	900	400	190		400	500						400		
SUPER VALVE	G	7	900	400	100	100	400	400								
W. BLACK	H	10	900	200	100	100	200	400							500	
YMAN-NEWD	B	20	800	200	200	280	200	400					350	350		
QUALITY ELECT	A	6	800	440			400	400								
RED VALVES	D	6	600	400			400				600					
TOTALS CARRIED FORWARD			24750					3200	5400	5150	1150	2470	2150	2100	750	450	600

CUSTOMER	INDUSTRY CATEGORY	MINIMUM CALLS NEEDED IN YEAR	TOTAL FORECAST	FORECAST SPREAD				PRODUCT GROUP BREAKDOWN									
				FIRST QUARTER	SECOND QUARTER	THIRD QUARTER	FOURTH QUARTER	0	1	2	3	4	5	6	7	8	9
TOTALS BROUGHT FORWARD																	
PNEUMATIC K'UP	C	4	400	200			200		300	100				100			
DAVIS SEARS	C	4	400	100	100	100	100		200					200			
AUTOLIFT	B	5	350	150	50	50	150				100		100			100	
WHITTAKER	A	6	250	100	50	50	150						350				
SEMBREENY	E	3	300	100	100	100	100							100	100	100	100
RUGBY PRECS	B	4	200	150			160							200	100		
APPLEGATE	A	6	300	100	50	50	100			100			100	100			
F. BERWICK	E	3	250	100		50	100	250					100	100			
WAKEFIELDS	C	4	250	150	50	50	50		100		50			50	50		
AP. MOTORS	F	3	200	100	50	60	50		100		100		60	100			
C. ELECTRICS	F	4	200	50	50	60	50		100	100	100			100			
N. TIPPETT	E	2	200	100			100			100					50	50	
TOTALS CARRIED FORWARD																	

Figure 5. Example of a sales forecast form for individual salesmen.

SALES FORECAST — USERS & KNOWN PROSPECTS

SALESMAN	MINIMUM CALLS NEEDED IN YEAR	TOTAL FORECAST	FORECAST SPREAD			
			FIRST QUARTER	SECOND QUARTER	THIRD QUARTER	FOURTH QUARTER
J. WATSON	766	65,150	24.050	12,500	10,500	18,100
R. BRIGGS	764	60,250	22,000	12,000	10,000	16,250
L. SUTTON	780	49,850	18,000	10,000	2,000	12,500
F. WINTERS	705	56,350	21,350	12,500	10,500	16,000
G. HOPGOOD	841	56,000	30,000	12,500	10,000	13,500
A. ROLFE	710	54,400	19,500	10,500	8,500	12,000
B. STONE	725	58,000	30,950	12,000	10,250	14,500
J. WOOD	742	19,000	19,000	12,500	10,000	15,000
O. BINNS	705	56,009	18,500	10,500	2,000	12,000
M. WHITE	822	74,500	26,000	15,000	12,500	24,000
TOTALS	7560	549,509	229,350	120,000	86,250	153,850

Figure 6. Example of a sales forecast form for the total company.

	TURNOVER EXPECTED FROM EACH PRODUCT GROUP								
0	1	2	3	4	5	6	7	8	9
,200	14,150	12,600	4,100	6,000	10.000	5,650	2,150	1,500	1,100
650	15,200	10,500	3,550	5,400	8,250	5,000	2,000	450	950
500	12,500	9.200	2,250	5,000	2,500	6,250	1,500	1,250	700
800	13,250	10,200	1,750	5,750	8,650	6,200	1,800	1,000	850
500	16,000	10,000	1,850	5,500	8,000	5,250	1,350	800	800
,000	12,150	9,500	2,200	6,500	2,500	4,500	2,000	1,500	1,650
450	11,700	10,250	2,750	6,000	7,750	5,750	2,900	1,200	650
,000	16,000	10,500	2,250	6,000	7,500	5,500	2,000	3,000	750
,000	10,500	11,000	2,800	5,000	7,000	1,000	1,850	1,250	500
,500	18,200	16,500	2,500	7,500	12,000	6,000	1,550	450	1,250
2600	139650	110250	26000	58,650	72150	51100	19050	12800	9200

Growth

Every company needs growth, otherwise it dies very quickly or is devoured by its competitors.

There are four ways for the average company to secure growth:

1 Increase its share of existing markets with its existing products, normally at the expense of its competitors (market penetration).
2 Find and develop *new* markets for its existing products (market development).
3 Develop *new* products which can be sold to existing markets (product development).
4 Diversification – usually by acquisition.

Most sales managers are concerned mainly with 1 and 2. Some take partial interest in 3. Few get involved in 4 – that's left to the board of directors (but who makes recommendations to the board, and on what criteria do acquisitions take place?).

Growth is *not* achieved by simply increasing prices, nor by maintaining one's market share in an expanding market. Yet still many practising managers fall into these traps, and think things are going well when really they are rapidly losing ground.

The Five-Year Plan

Not long ago, I came upon a company – well respected in its field – that had just put the finishing touches to its next five-year plan.

Turnover projections were based on an objective of approximately 25 per cent growth per year over the five years. Current turnover was £500,000, and the projection looked like this:

First year turnover	£ 500,000
Second year turnover	£ 625,000
Third year turnover	£ 800,000
Fourth year turnover	£ 975,000
Fifth year turnover	£1,250,000
Sixth year turnover	£1,500,000

A new factory extension was allowed for in the plan to cope with future production, but there was no provision whatever for new product development, and apart from plans to increase the secretarial staff of the sales office at strategic points along the turnover progression, the only other consideration given to the sales operation's part in this planned expansion was to budget for the employment of one extra salesman for every £100,000 increment of new turnover. The £100,000 figure was decided on because the average turnover currently achieved by each of the existing salesmen was between £80,000 and £100,000 per year.

The directors of this particular company were happily looking forward to the next five years, and were well content with the projected profit margins. They saw no insurmountable problems in finding the necessary number of new salesmen and training them up to effectiveness. They saw no shortfall developing in the market potential, or holdups through any failure to win slices of business from the competitors. They had even allowed for the costs of replacing some of their salesmen who might leave during the five-year period.

So when I suggested to these directors that the projected turnover could be achieved *without* the need to increase the size of the present sales force by even one man, you can in all probability imagine the cynical smiles I received. 'Humour him and he'll go away,' etc.

At least they gave me the opportunity to show them what I was thinking. '*If* prices increase 10 per cent a year during this next five years, what increase in turnover will this give the company without any other finger needed to be lifted ?'

Answer:

First year	£500,000
Second year	£550,000
Third year	£605,000
Fourth year	£665,500
Fifth year	£732,050
Sixth year	£805,255

'So you're a significant way towards your five year target on straight price increases alone,' I said.

Next question . . . 'What kind of personal development programme have you got for your salesmen?'

This question was greeted by a somewhat puzzled 'What do you mean?' 'Well,' I replied, 'if your salesmen are pulling in £100,000 worth of business this year, what scope are you going to give them for expanding on this? What encouragement for them to attain £120,000 next year? What back-up to make this attainment easier? What extra rewards if they move on to £200,000? What ongoing training to develop their knowledge of the products, the applications for the products and the markets for these applications?

'If your salesmen continue to pull in just £80,000 to £100,000 worth of business a year,' I continued, 'how long will it be, do you think, before they get fed up, lose that all-important job satisfaction, reckon they're in a rut and not getting anywhere – and quit?'

The puzzled frowns gradually turned to genuine surprise.

I rubbed some salt into the wound. 'To lose a good salesman and have to replace him at short notice would cost the company several months' new business turnover, the loss of a fair slice of goodwill, plus about £5,000 to train the new man up to full effectiveness. Even then, there would be some uncertainty – whether or not the new salesman will make the grade, and the cost of having to start all over again if he fails to make it.'

Surprise changing to a certain amount of apprehension.

'Wouldn't it be much more sensible to have some kind of planned personal development programme for each salesman, so that each man can develop his knowledge, his abilities, his territory, his customers, his sense of importance, his rewards based upon his own achievements – all this giving him the job satisfaction and pride that will keep him working effectively for you for many years to come?'

Nods and raised eyebrows.

'If, for example, each salesman could increase his turnover by 15 per cent per year, in true terms, price increases excluded, and if he were to be rewarded accordingly in addition to his usual salary increases linked to the cost of living index, do you think this would provide him with some significant job satisfaction?'

Emphatic affirmatives, 'more than some of 'em are worth' comments.

'So how does this 15 per cent personal improvement target linked to your calculated 10 per cent price increases per year, influence your five year turnover projection?'

The answer, of course, is obvious. The company could reach its £1½ million target with no additional salesmen, and with much less risk of losing the salesmen it already employed. Profits significantly increased. Problems significantly reduced.

The five-year plan was amended forthwith.

Will the Salesmen do it on their own?

It wouldn't have been fair to leave those directors with their revised five-year plan, just at that stage. So a few more questions were submitted.

'Would you have confidence in your present sales force achieving a 15 per cent per year increase in true turnover on their own – without supervision, without encouragement, without help, or without you at least monitoring the results as they happen?'

Heavy sighs, 'thought it would be too good to be true' comments.

'So how are you going to make sure it all happens? How are you going to monitor and measure your salesmen's performance as the months and the years go by, to make sure the desired improvement is achieved? How are you going to establish what back-up is necessary, and in what area of the country, or in what sector of the market or section of the product range? How are you going to calculate the amount of advertising and mail shots required in each territory, to generate the kind of response each salesman needs in order to make his "new business" target attainable without tears or frustration, or weeks of door-knocking? How are you going to make sure each salesman does the selling part of his job as effectively as possible, and the planning part of his job as efficiently as possible? How are you going to pinpoint problems in any salesman's effectiveness, quickly – so that you can rectify the problems just as quickly and stay on target? How are you going to get the salesmen to monitor their own territories so that they keep you fully aware of how the market is doing so that you don't miss out on any potential business?'

Hands in the air. 'Stop, stop. We haven't the time to do all that. Our sales manager can't even spare the time to get out in the field with his salesmen more than once or twice a month. He's already inundated with more paperwork than he can handle.'

'But does the paperwork he handles at present give him all the information I have just mentioned? And in a form which makes it easy to use? If his reporting and control system is really working for him it shouldn't need to take more than one hour a week of his time. My guess is that most of the paperwork with which he gets loaded at present isn't really necessary, or doesn't really do the job it was intended to do.

Most sales forces will not achieve any meaningful improvement in performance on their own. In fact, the reverse is true. Left to their own devices, most salesmen will gradually decline in performance. Every sales force needs a strong, determined, dedicated, enthusiastic sales manager. A leader. A manager who really manages. A man who can achieve results through the efforts of other people – his team. Not a promoted salesman who still thinks of himself as a salesman.

'And that sales manager, that team leader, must have at his fingertips all the information, figures, ratios, statistics, which will enable him to plan his next move, and the shape of the improvement target for each individual salesman in his team.'

'What kind of information ?' the directors demanded.

'How many days a year are available to the sales force for actual selling ?

'How many face-to-face calls can they make ?

'Which existing customers are worth calling on in the next year, which ones are not, and why are they and aren't they ?

'How much business will each of these existing customers produce next year ?

'How many calls will the sales force need to make to secure this repeat business ?

'How much time does the sales force have available to seek *new* business ?

'What proportion of the total business comes from quotations ?

'What is the conversion ratio of quotations into orders ?

'What is the average order value for (*a*) repeat business and (*b*) new business ?

'How many quotations must be generated to get to target ?

'What is each salesman's average miles per call ratio ?

'How many of each salesman's calls are made by appointment ?'

After an hour's discussion and quite a few internal telephone calls, the directors had to admit that their company could make a reasonable guess at four of these twelve questions. But only a guess. No one was actually recording any data from which a precise figure could be derived. This appeared to worry them.

'You have a significant element of "fudge factor" in your sales operation,' I stated.

'Fudge factor ?' the directors chorused. 'Fudge factor ? What the hell do you mean by that ?'

Fudge Factor

'Fudge factor,' I submitted, 'is the result of management not insisting on their sales force accepting and working to the same kind of disciplines expected of production, accounts, transport and most other departments in the company.'

Fudge factor is a term coined by Philip Lund, author of

Compelling Selling and *Sales Reports, Records and Systems*. Lund's words on the subject are as follows.

I have always found it hard to understand why people who run successful businesses consistently allow themselves to be betrayed by their field sales forces. For some strange reason, these otherwise competent executives accept a level of fudge factor from their sales operation that they would not tolerate from the other departments of their business.

In sales planning, targets and performance can be quantified and controls can be exercised through numbers just as easily as they can in production or in management accounting. The problem most businesses have had in the past, however, has been to discard existing outdated sales procedures and to replace them without disruption by a complete, yet simple, system that would rationalize their sales planning and control requirements.

No sales control system can replace the function of good field sales management, of course, but with the right system, this management will undoubtedly become much more efficient.

As with most managements struggling to see the light for the first time, a few comparisons had to be made to emphasize the fact that fudge factor existed, and ran rampant through their organization.

'Let's look at customer records,' I suggested. 'Would you allow your accountant to jot down his accounts in a little black book and take them with him when he leaves your employ?

'Would you allow your production blueprints to be just casual sketches, and again taken away to another company when a draughtsman leaves?

'So what happens when one of your salesmen leaves? Do you get back from him, before he goes, all his records and personal information on the customers and prospects in his territory? And if you do, are these records such that you can give them to his successor so that the new man can get his teeth into the job with the minimum of disruption of your sales effort?

'In fact, do you actually have a standard customer record system which you provide for your salesmen, or do you expect each man to devise and operate his own system?'

The silence was deafening.

ACTION TIME

Tick the applicable column

	Yes	No
1 Do you provide your salesmen with a standardized method for keeping customer records?		
2 Do your salesmen keep their customer records up to date — and *USE* them?		
3 Do you make sure a salesman who leaves the company doesn't take his customer records with him?		
4 Do you know how much prospecting work your salesmen need to do to achieve the company's 'New Business' target?		
5 If you can answer 'Yes' to question 4, do you know if your salesmen are actually *doing* the amount of prospecting work required?		
6 Do you receive a detailed plan from your salesmen of where they will be next week?		
7 Are more than 40% of your salesmen's calls 'By Appointment'?		
8 Do you know how much business your salesmen are chasing that your company has quoted for?		
9 Do you know how much of this business is likely to result in firm orders NEXT MONTH?		
10 Do your salesmen prepare for you a forecast of how much business they reckon they will produce for the company during the next period?		
11 Is this forecast in a sufficiently detailed form so that you can pinpoint any specific customer that isn't coming up to expectations?		
12 Are the action reports you receive from your salesmen sufficiently legible, detailed and accurate for the company to produce a quotation and be certain it will fulfil the customer's requirements?		
13 Do your salesmen submit a weekly report of the customers they have called upon — and what happened?		
14 If the answer to question 13 is 'Yes', does anyone use the information on the weekly reports, rather than just file them away after a general check?		
15 Do you know if any salesmen are neglecting part of your product range?		
16 Do you know your company's average order value?		
17 Do you know your company's 'calls to quotations' ratio?		
18 Do you know your company's 'quotations to orders' ratio?		
Totals		

Figure 7.

'Let's look at forward planning,' I continued.

'Do you demand from your accounts department a financial plan that enables the company to maintain adequate cash flow?

'Do you expect production to know what they are going to produce next week?

'Do you allow your delivery vans to go where they please?

'So do you get from your salesmen a plan of where they intend to go next week? And, more important, what they intend to do when they get there?

'Production knows its capacity, yet how many of your salesmen have worked out their *order capacity* for the next twelve months?

'If I may add a question on quality control . . .

'Doubless you take note of the amount of wastage of materials in your factory, and of the number of rejects and the scrap rates. Your accounts department is also keeping a close watch on all outstanding invoices, to make sure every customer pays his bills within a reasonable time. All the products in the factory are subjected to strict quality control and testing.

'But to what extent does your sales manager measure, inspect, and test the quality of his salesmen's performance?'

'Enough!' cried the directors. 'What do you suggest we do?'

'Well, the first thing to do,' I replied, 'is to try to establish the extent to which "fudge factor" has taken a grip on your sales organization.'

I handed each director a checklist. 'Answer the eighteen questions [as listed in figure 7], and then let's see what we can do to rectify all the "Nos".'

Any reader who logs more than six Nos on this checklist has a few major problems to solve. Read the section on Personal performance to find out how to start measuring all these things with the minimum of paperwork and time commitment.

Holes (sudden)

One of the biggest problems a sales manager faces is having one of his salesmen suddenly quit without warning, leaving him with a large hole which has to be filled up before customer service suffers too much.

Only the largest companies can afford to take on one or two young trainees, and be developing their potential in the sales office ready for a sudden hole to appear. Most sales managers have to draft a quick advertisement and hope for the best.

Two things you can do to reduce the problem:

1 Do some regular detective work and build up a file of personal contacts who might make good salesmen if and when the need arises. These might be salesmen working for other companies (but please, not your direct competitors) or even a few of your customers who yearn for the outdoor life and have the requisite temperament, abilities and motivation. Then just a phone call could get you the new man you need.
2 Hold regular meetings with the other department heads in your company, and try to establish a procedure for growing your own new salesmen, fertilizing them (covering their costs) through the jobs they are doing in the other departments of the company. The one factor against this, of course, is the sudden hole a man leaves in another department when he moves to sales. But holes in design, production, commercial, service, etc. are usually easier to fill or patch over than holes in sales.

If in Doubt - Ask

Every sheet of drawing paper used in every drawing office in British industry has these words printed on it in large letters: *If in doubt – ask*.

No designer or engineer would ever dream of committing himself to something of a technical nature unless he was sure. So why doesn't the same principle apply to the sales office ?

Half the quotations sent to customers by suppliers are inaccurate in some way, mainly because the instructions received from the salesman were incomplete or illegible.

And rarely, if ever, does the sales office throw the instruction back at the salesman and ask him to do it again, or fill in the gaps. Instead, the sales office tries to interpret the instructions as best it can.

And another potential order is lost.

Make your sales office different. Make everyone operate under those fundamental words on the drawing paper: *If in doubt – ask*.

Make it easy for your salesmen to provide the information the sales office needs. Get the salesmen using checklists and properly designed forms for their action requests like the one shown in figure 8.

And give your sales office manager the authority to send things back to the salesmen and tell them to do the job properly. The problem will then soon disappear.

ACTION REQUEST	SALESMAN _J. WATSON_	
COMPANY'S FULL NAME _P.K. VALVES (1972) Ltd_		DATE OF CALL

FULL ADDRESS INCL. POSTAL CODE _HANLEY WORKS_ _UPTON LANE WARELEY BM41_	CONTACT'S NAME / INITIALS _W.F. EVANS_ POSITION IN COMPANY _ASST PLANT BUYER_

PLEASE REQUOTE ON BASIS OF
OUR QUOTE No 4267 (RT) OF JULY 17th
BUT PROVIDE FOR :—

(A) MULTI-SPINDLE ATTACHMENT (TTA)

(B) DOUBLE SET OF TOOLS & 2 SPARES
KITS

(C) PROVIDE FOR ESTIMATED PRICE
INCREASES BY MARCH NEXT YEAR
(DATE OF CLIENT'S DECISION TO PURCHASE)

COMPETITION

ALL USUAL U.K. COMPANIES PLUS
SPIEGEL GambH, Essen Germany

ANYTHING ATTACHED NO

ACTION _VITAL BEFORE OCT 31st_ _BOARD MEETING OF CLIENT WILL_ _DECIDE 1st sorting OF TENDERS ON_ _Nov 2nd_	DEADLINE _OCT. 31st._
SEND EVERYTHING TO THE SALESMAN	SEND DIRECT TO THE CONTACT NAMED ABOVE ▶ ✗	HQ REPLAY TO SALESMAN IF PROBLEMS FAST

Figure 8. Example of a salesman's action request form.

> # PRAY GIVE ME A COMPREHENSIVE REPORT ON ONE SIDE ONLY OF STANDARD MEMORANDUM PAPER
>
> ## WINSTON S. CHURCHILL

Interdepartmental Relationships

Most companies have more problems communicating between their own departments than they do communicating with their customers and suppliers. Probably it's because so much is taken for granted by so many.

If you want to have some fun and at the same time get your interdepartmental communications straightened out, circulate the checklist shown in figure 9 to all department heads, with a memo saying:

Please can we discuss your findings on the attached checklist at our next monthly management meeting.

You'll find at the next meeting that everyone has blamed everyone else. Let the discussion rage for half an hour, and then quietly ask everyone at the meeting to reflect on the past thirty minutes. You'll have to take some of the blame, of course, just like all the others.

J

Job Specifications and Job Descriptions

Would you believe that the majority of people in selling and sales management don't have either?

A job description is like a compass – it points you in the right direction and keeps you there. Try steering a ship without a compass.

Any sales manager without a job description should at once set about writing his own, then submit it to the powers that be for approval, or modification and then approval.

A sales manager taking on new salesmen begins with a job specification – a negotiating document used to make sure the applicant fits all the key tasks required of him – or most of them. Once taken on, this job specification is redrafted to include the specific detail on individual performance standards expected and then becomes that individual applicant's job description.

If a sales manager has to draft job descriptions from scratch for an existing sales force, the best method is to get every salesman to draft his own, then pool the results and have the sales manager *only* develop the final format and the individual detailed contents for each salesman (remember the camel which was a horse designed by a committee).

Sample Job Specification/Description for a Salesman

Job title: Sales engineer.
Responsible to: UK sales manager.

	N/A	YES	NO	PAR	?	ACT
1 In relation to other departments which of the following are causing delays or problems in my departments and should be discussed at management meetings?						
(a) Relevant information not being transmitted by other departments?						
(b) Incomplete information received from other departments?						
(c) Work flow interruptions caused by constant requests for immediate action or information?						
(d) Formal lines of communication being ignored or by-passed?						
(e) Verbal communications lacking in clarity — resulting in misunderstandings and misinterpretation?						
(f) Requests for action/information not complied with?						
(g) Impaired efficiency due to forgetfulness by other departments?						
(h) A build up of frustration caused by poor communications between departments?						
2 If I prepare specific recommendations on ways and means to improve any of the above are they likely to be accepted and complied with?						
3 If 'No' or 'Query', can I indicate the loss of efficiency caused by any particular shortcoming(s)?						
4 . . . . and thus gain acceptance and co-operation?						
5 Have we recently studied our methods and lines of communications and assessed the present weaknesses in relation to future expansion?						
6 If no, should we seek suggestions from departments upon improvements or communications?						

8 Is any one person or department persistently lacking in good communications?

9 If yes, have they been made fully aware of the problems that are being created?

10 Are we inclined to rely too heavily upon verbal communications?

11 If yes, should we assess which verbal communications are frequently inadequate?

12 .... and apply written communications to overcome this?

13 Have we studied which repetitive communications affect more than one person or department?

14 ... and considered the simplest and quickest method of imparting the information to all concerned?

15 Could important requests and replies be conveyed via internal memo's?

16 .... which also indicate the degree of urgency?

17 .... supported by a 'bring-up' procedure for those requests which require acknowledgement, answer or action?

18 Are documents date-stamped by departments to show dates of receipt and completion?

19 .... to indicate the total time taken to process.

20 Are documents coded to indicate the degree of priority?

21 .... and the need for feed-back information?

22 Is the principal of 'do it now' sufficiently instilled in managers and staff?

Figure 9. A communications checklist.

Sales area: The sales area known as area Number 5 comprising the counties of Kent, Sussex, and Surrey.

Purpose: To maintain and develop business with existing customers in the area and to develop business by locating and selling to new outlets in the area.

Prime Duties and Responsibilities

1 To acquire a thorough working knowledge of all the company's products and a thorough understanding of all their applications.

To keep this knowledge up to date through regular sales meetings and product training sessions held monthly at HQ.

Performance will be considered satisfactory when full selling proposals, including detailed financial justification, can be drafted for all customer applications to be found in area Number 5.

2 To acquire and develop all necessary professional selling skills through the meetings and training sessions referred to in (1), through attendance at outside sales training courses in accordance with the company's personal development programmes and by discussion, reading, and constant practice.

Performance will be considered satisfactory when all eight personal performance ratios are consistently better than the company norms for these ratios, and all factors on the monthly personal selling standards record are consistently marked 'above standard'.

3 To plan the coverage of the area in the most effective and economic manner.

Performance will be considered satisfactory when:

(a) All customer and prospective customer records are up to date and contain full information on names, initials and positions of all contacts, best day and time to call on each contact, name of secretary, and contain a properly reported call record which specifies in all cases the aim of the *next* call and the firm date of the next call.

(b) These customer and prospective customer records can be used to produce a forecast of future business expected from the area which is subsequently proved accurate.

(c) A cycle-of-calling plan is in existence for the area and is being worked in a systematic manner.

(d) A list of live new business prospects is being properly researched every month, prior to calling, the number of prospects on each monthly list being consistent with the known requirement for that time which has been calculated from the personal performance ratios.

(e) At all times there is an adequate list of prospects in negotiation and that steady movement towards conclusion can be demonstrated.

(f) A fully detailed call plan, itemizing all calls to be made during the following week and with at least 60 per cent of these calls having firm appointments, is received every Friday by the UK sales manager.

4 To report coherently and with speed and economy of words on day-to-day activities, customer installations, prevailing or changing business trends, customer complaints and satisfaction and competitors' activity, such reporting to be in accordance with directives issued from time to time by the UK sales manager and on the appropriate forms supplied for these purposes.

5 Attendance at all regional sales meetings, national sales meetings, and company-organized training sessions is mandatory.

6 To liaise whenever necessary with the sales office manager, chief draughtsman, development manager, production manager and chief accountant to ensure a proper level of customer service and customer advice is maintained.

7 To develop relationships with customers that further the goodwill attaching to the company name.

Performance in this respect will be considered satisfactory when sales demonstrations to prospects take place at existing customers' premises in the area on a regular basis and the reception given to company personnel when visiting customers in the area is seen to generally reflect this goodwill.

8 The prime objective will be met when sales in the area by total, rate and product mix equate with the forecasts prepared for and the targets set for the area.

Sample Job Specification for a UK Sales Manager

Job title: UK sales manager.

Responsible to: Managing director (this sample assumes the company has no sales or marketing director).

Responsible for: All UK sales activities.

Staff responsible for: All UK sales engineers,

sales office manager,
service manager,
product managers (if any),
technical services manager,
marketing services (including publicity).

Main purpose of job: To control and coordinate the UK sales and marketing activities of the company, based at the company's head office, and to ensure the highest possible profitability at the correct balance of product sales, the efficient operation of the sales department and maximum job satisfaction for the personnel employed therein and for whom the UK sales manager is directly responsible.

Main Duties and Responsibilities

1 To advise the board of directors on all matters of policy relating to UK sales and marketing.

2 To direct and manage the sales department within the policies laid down by the board of directors.

3 To liaise with the export sales manager on use of the technical services department and the marketing services department for export activities.

(I've accepted a long-standing British tradition here, that export is the 'poor relation' of home sales. I don't like it, and I'm firmly convinced that if British companies applied the same volume of manpower to export that they do to home sales, this country's problems would be over.)

4 To liaise with product managers and discuss, agree, and implement variations in product sales policies whenever established necessary.

5 To arbitrate on all serious disagreements with customers, if necessary enlisting the managing director's help, and to bring all such disagreements to the speediest possible conclusion which is satisfactory to the customer.

6 In conjunction with the board of directors and the personnel manager, to establish salary formulae and commission formulae to meet the needs of the sales personnel, bearing in mind the objective of matching maximum profitability to maximum job satisfaction.

7 To prepare and submit to the board of directors the annual and long-range expenditure and capital budgets for those departments for which the UK sales manager is responsible,

and likewise all sales forecasts relating to annual and long range product sales.

8 To monitor continuously actual costs against budgeted costs, and actual sales against budgeted sales for the UK sales operation.

9 To ensure that a congenial working environment is maintained within all departments for which the UK sales manager is responsible.

10 To undertake all interviews and selection of new staff for the sales force.

11 To ensure that all employees for whom the UK sales manager is responsible receive adequate training to fit them for the jobs they are employed to do.

12 To chair all product planning meetings.

13 To direct and control UK product strategy.

14 To direct and control UK marketing strategy.

15 To control product mix with appropriate liaison with the production manager and with regard to the objective of maximum profitability.

16 To prepare a monthly report on UK sales activity for the board of directors.

17 To spend at least one day per month in the field with each of the UK sales engineers, to assess the sales engineer's performance and progress and to give any assistance necessary to assure steady progress.

18 To monitor UK sales activities and assure that satisfactory performance levels are maintained for the sales force as a whole and for each sales engineer individually.

19 To recommend and implement changes in manpower structure and control where necessary within the UK sales operation.

20 To ensure that effective disciplinary procedures are in force and carried out within the UK sales operation.

21 To carry out such additional duties as may become necessary from time to time to ensure the smooth running of the UK sales operation.

As you can probably see, the sales manager's job *specification* is a shade more all-enveloping than the salesman's. There are so many varieties of sales managers in British industry that it is impossible to standardize. Thus, my sample is for guideline purposes only. Here is part of a sales manager's detailed job *description*, listing his performance standards.

Job description: Sales manager
Reports to: Managing director
Main responsibility: The attainment of sales objectives through the effective operation of the field sales force.

Sales Objectives

Organizes, leads, trains, motivates, and controls the sales force to ensure the on-time attainment of sales objectives, and in particular, the attainment of:

1 Sales targets by product.
2 Sales targets by territory.
3 Sales targets by key customers.
4 Sales activity by region.
5 Sales activity by territory.

Standards of performance relative to the above are attained when:

1 The national annual sales target is attained.
2 When the number of salesmen not attaining target is below 15 per cent of the field force.
3 When more than 80 per cent of the key accounts have attained or surpassed the agreed target figure.
4 When the national average effective call rate is 6 per man per day.
5 When the inquiry to call ratio is less than 1 to 7 and is seen to be reducing.
6 When the number of product demonstrations average at least 3 per man per day.
7 When the number of 'orders on the spot' averages at least 5 per man per week, and increasing.
8 When the order to call ratio is less than 1 to 8 and reducing.
9 When the order to inquiry ratio is less than 1 to $1\frac{1}{2}$.
10 When the average value of order is £250 and increasing.
11 When the number of calls made on new prospects averages at least 5 per man per week.
12 When the number of calls made upon dormant accounts averages at least 2 per man per week.
13 When the cost per call is less than £10.
14 When the average gross margin is held to 15 per cent minimum.
15 When the direct sales cost is held at or below 12.5 per cent.

Just for the sales manager who is faced with the task of selling the concept of job specifications and descriptions to his managing director, here is a sample for a managing director.

Sample Job Specification for a Managing Director

Job title:	Managing director, UK Widgets Ltd.
Reporting to:	Vice-president Marketing, Universal Widget Corporation.
Liaising with:	Moulded Widgets Ltd (managing director), Widgets SA France (managing director), Widgets Gmbh (managing director).
Function:	Overall responsibility for the profitable management of UK Widgets Ltd.
Geographic area:	All UK and Eire.
Group management meetings:	Attendance at monthly management meetings with associate group companies is mandatory.

Duties

1 **Marketing** To achieve a high market share in volume and value.

To maximize price levels consistent with market share and volume.

To appraise constantly and update marketing polices.

To review economic data relevant to markets on a consistent basis.

To review market trends, competitive activity and general market data.

To develop and update all advertising, promotional activities and product literature.

To maintain customer service in respect of sales administration, distribution stocks and spares inventory, relative to sales forecasts.

To develop sound relationships with relevant trade associations, professional and technical bodies operating in the UK.

To develop sales for present products into new markets.

To obtain and maintain a wide range of live business contacts.

To provide vigour in the sales force.

2 **Financial** To ensure that all company activities are co-ordinated by the financial controller and that all reports and returns required by company law are filed in due time.

To maintain under strict surveillance all cost/profit contributions on a regular basis.

To keep a watching brief on cost trends.

To control and anticipate overhead expenses using planned budgets.

To ensure all costing systems have instant update.

To review debtors on a minimum monthly basis.

To control inventory levels.

To provide adequate space for planned inventory.

To shed unprofitable products.

To maintain the group's price leadership philosophy.

To produce all necessary budgets and forecasts.

3 **Production/Product Development** To maintain and enhance product quality.

To ensure that production units (own and subcontract) have sales forecasts.

To maintain a review of end users and specifiers of Widgets in all markets.

To improve present range of products.

To develop a more effective produce mix.

To develop a more effective market mix.

To develop new products for new markets.

To coordinate existing products and new products.

4 To ensure that a monthly report covering marketing, finance and production/product development is submitted to the vice-president marketing.

5 **Purchasing** To ensure that products and materials required for UK Widgets Ltd are procured from reliable, cost-effective and technically competent sources.

6 **Personnel** To recruit management personnel and to delegate to them duties as required.

To attract to and maintain at UK Widgets Ltd top-quality management and staff.

To remunerate and motivate above-average people at above-average levels as an investment in long-term performance.

To develop future managers for expanding operations elsewhere in Universal Widget Corporation.

To maintain a good working environment.

To update terms and conditions of employment in line with current legislation.

To develop on a continuous basis an improved organizational structure.

7 **Legal** To take appropriate legal advice on all relevant matters, and to refer to fellow directors and vice-president marketing on these relevant matters.

To be watchful and defensive of the company's patents, registered designs, copyrights and trade names.

To maintain a strictly legal posture in dealing with employees, suppliers, customers, trade unions, local authorities and government departments.

8 **Planning** To ensure that adequate medium and long-range plans are produced for products in: (a) the motor vehicle widget market, (b) the aerospace widget market, (c) the civil engineering widget market.

To perceive new needs and opportunities and to prepare and submit plans accordingly to the vice-president marketing.

Managing directors who also perform the function of sales manager need to knit these last two sample job specifications together to make one. You want any better reason to start looking for a sales manager? It's better than a coronary.

Kerbside Conferences

Why do most sales managers avoid regularly spending a day with each of their salesmen, making just ordinary calls ? It isn't just because they are always too busy. I think it is because a clear-cut objective for the day's visit has never been established and so there is a feeling of embarrassment between manager and salesman and often a feeling on the part of the salesman that his manager is only checking up on him.

Which he is. But there is a right way and a wrong way to check up.

Here's a way for you to make these days out with the salesmen as effective as possible and banish all that bad feeling. The illustrations shown in figures 10 and 11 are of a document used by firms like Ross Foods Ltd and GKN Sankey Automatic Vending Division to keep their salesmen and their sales managers really on their toes. The document, called *Personal selling standards and performance record*, forms the basis for a one-day-per-month field visit, with both salesman and manager clearly understanding what is expected. On each field visit, the manager assesses the salesman on twenty-four different aspects of his job. At the end of the day, they both get together for a kerbside conference on the day's activities and *agree* the assessments.

Then salesman and manager agree together what action the salesman needs to take in the ensuing month, to improve any aspects that are below par. One month later, they can see what improvement has occurred – and so on. Main aim – to have all twenty-four aspects consistently above standard.

SELLING SKILLS

	ABOVE STANDARD	STANDARD	NEEDS IMPROVEMENT
1 PLANNING PREPARATION			
a) Information	Has all the relevant information for every call	Has most of the relevant information for every call	Has some relevant information for most calls
b) Sales tools	Always carried all relevant equipment, stationery etc.	Invariably carried some relevant equipment, stationery etc.	Often carried some relevant equipment, stationery etc.
c) Action plan	Always prepared detailed action plan	Invariably prepares action plan	Often prepares an action plan
2 APPROACH			
a) Opening remarks	Always gains attention by using skilful opening phrases and "carrots"	Occasionally fails to gain attention because of failure to use "carrots"	Seldom uses "carrots" or skilful opening phrases
b) Sales aids	Always uses a sales aid where appropriate	Often uses a sales aid in approach	Seldom uses a sales aid in approach
3 PRESENTATION			
a) Product knowledge	Fully conversant with all products and applications	Well informed about all products and applications	Has some knowledge of most products and applications
b) Selling points	Knows and uses all selling points for all products	Knows most selling points for all products	Knows some selling points for most products
c) Buyer benefits	Always translates selling points into benefits	Occasionally fails to translate selling points into benefits	Sometimes translates selling points into benefits
d) Buying motives	Always makes presentation appeal to buyers motives	Occasionally fails to make presentation appeal to buyers motives	Often fails to make presentation appeal to buyers motives
e) Sales aids	Always uses them to maximum advantage	Always uses them, often to maximum advantage	Sometimes uses sales aids, to advantage
f) Handling objections	Always handles objections successfully, leaving the buyer satisfied	Handles most objections successfully leaving the buyer satisfied	Handles some objections successfully, does not always leave the buyer satisfied
g) Selling sequence	Always uses correct sequence	Often uses correct sequence	Seldom uses correct sequence
h) Rental	Always endeavours to sell Rental	Often endeavours to sell Rental	Seldom endeavours to sell Rental
4 CLOSING THE SALE			
a) Buying signals	Always recognises and acts upon buying signals	Occasionally fails to recognise and act upon buying signals	Often fails to recognise and act upon buying signals
	Always uses the most appropriate style of close	Occasionally fails to use the appropriate style of close	Often fails to use the appropriate style of close
c) Departure drill	Always thanks, reassures or questions buyer as appropriate	Occasionally fails to thank, reassure or question the buyer as appropriate	Often fails to thank, reassure or question the buyer as appropriate

Figure 10. A guide to the salesman's performance appraisal record form shown in figure 11.

	ABOVE STANDARD	STANDARD	NEEDS IMPROVEMENT
5 CALL ANALYSIS			
a) Records/reports and Correspondence	Always completed accurately, promptly and up to date	Occasionally fails to complete accurately, promptly and up to date	Always completed but not always accurate, prompt and up to date
b) Information	Always records information for future use	Occasionally fails to record information for future use	Sometimes records information for future use
c) Self analysis	Invariably analyses personal performance	Often analyses personal performance	Seldom analyses personal performance
6 TERRITORY MANAGEMENT			
a) Use of selling time	Plans very carefully and wastes no time	Plans carefully, and wastes little time	Does not plan, and wastes time on unnecessary journeys
b) Competitors Activities	Actively seeks relevant information and keeps everybody informed	Generally good at reporting information	Seldom reports competitor activity
c) Territory Development	Constantly active and opening new a/cs in addition to developing existing a/cs	Developing existing a/cs and Occasionally opening new a/cs	Inclined to concentrate on existing business seldom trying to gain new customers
7 PERSONAL			
a) Appearance	Always exceptionally well turned out, and a credit to his company	Always well turned out and a credit to his company	Not always well turned out and a credit to the company
b) Attitude	Always expresses a positive attitude towards the company its products, policies, and its customers	Occasionally fails to express a positive attitude towards the company its products, policies, and its customers	Often expresses a negative attitude towards the company its products, policies and its customers
8 OTHER RELEVANT POINTS			

(continuation of figure 10)

ON-GOING PERSONAL SKILLS RECORD

By using the Performance Standards as a guide, rate performance under the following headings:
A = Above Standard B = Standard C = Needs Improvement

Date of appraisal																		
1 PLANNING PREPARATION																		
a) Information																		
b) Sales tools																		
c) Action plan																		
2 APPROACH																		
a) Opening remarks																		
b) Sales aids																		
3 PRESENTATION																		
a) Product knowledge																		
b) Selling points																		
c) Buyer benefits																		
d) Buying motives																		
e) Sales aids																		
f) Handling objections																		
g) Selling sequence																		
h) Rental																		
4 CLOSING THE SALE																		
a) Buying signals																		
b) Method of Close																		
c) Departure drill																		
5 CALL ANALYSIS																		
a) Records/reports/correspondence																		
b) Information																		
c) Self analysis																		
6 TERRITORY MANAGEMENT																		
a) Use of selling time																		
b) Competitors' activities																		
c) Territory development																		
7 PERSONAL																		
a) Appearance																		
b) Attitude																		
Appraisor's Signature																		

At the end of each appraisal day, the Sales Manager should complete this form, with the salesman, discussing the various areas where improvement is necessary in relation to the day's work. The Sales Manager should give recommendations and guidance on how the agreed weaknesses should be improved.
No allowances should be made for inexperience.

Figure 11. Example of a salesman's performance appraisal record form, to be used for continuous monitoring.

Two words of warning. During the day's calls, you must sit back and let the salesman do all the work. Don't let him introduce you as his boss, only as 'Mr— from HQ, out with me today as part of a familiarization exercise'. And when you start the kerbside conference, no recriminations. It's not a hatchet meeting.

Key Questions for Sales Managers

I keep six honest serving men
They taught me all I knew.
Their names are What and Why and When
And How and Where and Who.

                          Kipling

What?

What are my own personal objectives ?
What do I want to accomplish in life ?
What personal results am I trying to achieve ?
For what purpose ?

Why?

Why am I striving to do this ?
Why is it necessary ?
Does it have permanent value ?
Temporary value ?
Is it 100 per cent useful ?

When?

When is this going to be accomplished?
Long-range? Short-range?
What's the schedule?

How?

How am I going to accomplish my major objectives?
How can I improve my present performance?

Where?

Where have I been?
Where am I now?
Where am I going from here?

Who?

Who are my most helpful advisers?
And critics?
Who should be consulted about what problems?
Who is best qualified to do what?
Who are the outstanding leaders in my field?

Leadership

The most important quality of all for a sales manager.

Very difficult to define. Some people have it from childhood, others have to work very hard at the main ingredients that make a good leader of salesmen.

Here is a worklist for the hard-working:

1   A Good Memory

To enable him to recall people's names, and the few essential facts that are pertinent to a wide range of problems.

2   A Genuine Interest in People

Those for whom you are responsible for leading will know at once if you are genuinely interested in them and particularly in their development. Show this – and you create the personal bond that is essential to the success of your team.

You *cannot* fake an interest in people – they *always* find you out.

A leader can only be successful by ensuring the success of every individual in the team.

3   Integrity

If the team has cause to doubt the integrity of its leader, then it will fail when the team is exposed to stress or a risk.

If a man is capable of minor lapses in his personal integrity

– he fails to 'keep faith' – then he could let his own team members down when he is under pressure. Once the team doubts the leader – the doubt greatly limits their chances of the fullest success.

4 The Ability to Communicate Effectively

A good leader must be able to talk – and write – simply, clearly and persuasively. He must also listen – and digest information – intently. Communication is a two-way process.

5 Decisiveness

There comes a time when a decision must be made – and a risk taken – even though the facts may be incomplete.

A leader must recognize when further analyis is unprofitable and action is needed.

It helps if the cost of changing the decision is known. If the cost is low – the risk is low.

6 The Ability to Relax

If the team is kept tense, and under pressure, irritation arises and performance fails. This is overcome by deliberately introducing a 'break' – just a light remark or opportunity for laughter.

The importance lies in the frequency and the need for the 'break' to be related to the task or the people – not 'a funny story'. The break should be brief – even momentary. It should also come at an opportune moment.

7 Genuine Enthusiasm

Inner conviction – belief in the team and the objectives before it – give rise to enthusiasm. This *must* be visible to the members of the team. It provides the 'motive power' they use to tackle their jobs with courage and hope.

If the leader has no belief in the task – why should his team even attempt it ?

Leadswingers

If you develop a feeling in your water that one of your salesmen is not playing fair, then take positive action fast, otherwise the feeling will grow into a cancerous attitude against the man which will insidiously mar your working relationship.

Find out for sure whether he takes his kids to school each morning, collects them each afternoon, makes all the calls his reports say he has, plays golf with his mates alternate Wednesdays and Fridays or whatever.

And if he does, have him into your office and present him with the facts. Then tell him he's being a bloody fool, ask him to choose between resigning and doing the job properly, and if he decides to carry on confirm the discussion with a confidential memo.

Check again seven weeks later. If he's still leadswinging, or attending interviews for another job, fire him on the spot. No notice, no salary in lieu. Then call the rest of the team together and tell them all precisely what you have done and why. After that, no one's in any doubt about what will happen to leadswingers in this organization.

Of course, it follows that school trips, weekday golf, etc. are all out for you.

League Tables

Don't ever try to hide the company's true performance from your salesmen, or disguise money figures by allocating code numbers or units. Play it all straight; tell everyone the worst – and the best.

Give each salesman a detailed rundown of his sales figures, calls, quotations, leads, ratios, profitability and whatever at least once a month. Give each salesman everyone else's figures also. Let everyone see how everyone else is doing.

RESULTS AT END OF MONTH — 8				AREA MANAGER'S CURRENT ESTIMATE FOR REST OF YEAR		
SALESMAN	ORIGINAL AGREED ANNUAL TARGET	TURNOVER ACHIEVED SO FAR	BALANCE LEFT TO ACHIEVE	WILL MAKE BALANCE ON NOSE	WILL SELL MORE THAN BALANCE BY	WILL SELL LESS THAN BALANCE BY
ANDREWS, J.	150,000	98,000	52,000	✓		
ARNOLD, P.	150,000	122,000	28,000	✓		
BEASLEY, G.	110,000	108,000	2,000		25,000	
BREWSTER, M	110,000	85,000	25,000	✓		
CARVER, D.	84,000	61,000	23,000	✓		
EVANS, D.	110,000	73,000	37,000			20,000
GILLMAN, R.	140,000	80,000	60,000			25,000
JACOBS, E.	125,000	123,000	2,000		35,000	
KEITH, B.	80,000	58,000	22,000		5,000	
McEWAN, J.	86,000	35,000	51,000			33,000
NORMAN, L.	150,000	105,000	45,000	✓		
ONIONS, P.	127,000	90,000	37,000			17,000
PACKER, A.	165,000	122,000	43,000		10,000	
PORTER, J.	130,000	70,000	60,0C0			30,000
ROBERTS, G.	55,000	36,000	19,000	✓		
SUTCLIFFE,S.	102,000	75,000	27,000			7,000
TAYLOR, B.	60,000	37,000	23,000		7,000	
THOMPSON,P.	110,000	79,000	31,000		2,000	
VINCENT, W.	100,000	85,000	15,000		18,000	
WATSON, J.	150,000	110,000	40,000		5,000	

All figures rounded up or down to nearest 1000.

Figure 12. Example of a league table for salesmen.

Only then will you begin to convert the salesmen at the bottom of the league table into self-starters. All you need to do after that is keep filling the tank and priming the petrol pump.

The best kind of league table is one which relates to the annual targets and which allows the targets to be adjusted as the months progress (not the targets related to commission earnings). Figure 12 shows an example of such a league table for a company employing twenty salesmen and having four area sales managers who regularly reassess the business outlook for each of their salesmen.

Low-Potential Accounts

Eighty per cent of your repeat business will be coming from less than 20 per cent of your customers.

And 80 per cent of your salesmen's time they will be spending servicing customers who only bring in less than 20 per cent of the total repeat business, unless you mainly deal in 'one-offs'.

Facts of life – and facts which are quickly making the salesman a very expensive animal to have on the payroll.

It's a general dilemma right across industry. You cannot afford to allow your salesmen to call very often on low potential customers, and you cannot afford to lose that 20 per cent of turnover, because some of today's small fry will be tomorrow's medium and big customers.

The answer to the dilemma is to service repeat business from your low potential accounts by telephone, not by salesmen. Put together a telesales desk at each of your regional offices (if you have any) or do it from head office (the cost of the telephone calls will still be much lower than the cost of face-to-face calls).

The successful changeover from salesmen to telesales depends on you following these steps:

1 Tell your salesmen what you have in mind and why. Ask each of them to give you a list of the low potential customers whom they feel are suitable for the new telesales service. Impress upon the salesmen that no nasty or difficult customers should go on the list, only easy happy ones. Also impress upon the salesmen that any time one of these customers wants to see a salesman, a salesman will be allowed to call.

The easiest ever method of ordering small tools

For some time now we have been operating what we firmly believe to be today's most efficient and trouble-free tool ordering service. We supply the widest range of small tools currently available, most of the time delivered within 48 hours. All that is needed from you is one phone call to your Herbert Distribution Centre.

Now we're taking the ultimate step.

We've even managed to eliminate the phone call.

From now on we are offering to a carefully selected group of valued clients, a completely new ordering service. One which requires you to do nothing except answer the phone. Here's how it works.

After consultation with you, we will arrange to ring any number and extension you wish, talk to any individual you nominate at whatever times and on whatever dates you decide fits your system best.

We will contact you monthly, weekly, or whenever you like. We will call on a given day of the month, or on a selected day of the week. When we call, simply give us your order and the Herbert computerised ordering system will go into action, bringing your tools with the minimum of delay. Or you can simply say "Nothing today thanks!" and we'll ring off until next time.

Think of the advantages:
* No need to remember to ring us for tools.
* No chance of being held up by busy phone lines, or the vagaries of the post office.
* Constant communication with the most efficient tool service in Britain. With no effort from yourself.
* And a corresponding reduction in your phone bill.

To enjoy this service you need take no action. In a few days we will ring you to see if we can be of service.

If after due consideration you decide that this new service is not for you — tell us on our next call and we won't bother you with it again.

One last thing — if you join the 'Phone-in' service or not, you can always get top Herbert service by ringing your local Distribution Centre. Anytime.

Figure 13.

2 Allocate specific customers to specific telesales staff: make sure only the person allocated that customer ever telephones that customer, and then thoroughly train the telesales staff in telesales techniques and how to start the ball rolling. (Structured Training Ltd can help you there.)

3 Send each customer a specially designed package of literature, product stock lists, price lists, etc. to introduce the new telesales service like the example from Herbert Tooling Ltd shown in figure 13. Note carefully the text in this example.

4 Follow up the literature with the first telephone call a few days later. (A good telesales person never has a problem persuading even the most cynical and reluctant customer at least to give the new service a try. After all, he's got absolutely nothing to lose, or to do. All he can do is gain.)

Available Equipment

Post Office Telecommunications can make a telesales desk highly efficient. To back up the ordinary telephone you can instal a Card Callmaker system, so that your telesales person doesn't even have to look up and dial the number. (Ask for PO leaflet DLE 562.) Or a more sophisticated magnetic tape callmaker that will store up to 400 telephone numbers on one tape.

You can provide headsets which allow your telesales people to keep both hands free at all times. You can install a Key and Lamp system (PO leaflet DLE 580) which allows a number of telephones to be used on a number of outside lines, without the need for a central switchboard operator.

When the telesales system has been working smoothly and successfully for a year or so, you may like to get it doing a little more. Like handling a few *difficult* customers with whom the salesmen cannot get on.

Firms like Birds Eye, Ross Foods and Coca-Cola in the consumer sales side of the business now generate more than 80 per cent of their total sales through telesales operations.

Ross Foods have calculated that the all-in cost of a telesales call is one-third the cost of a face-to-face call by a salesman. The average length of a Ross telesales call is 3.7 minutes, compared with the average length of a face-to-face call of 20 minutes.

Average cost of a telesales call (all-in costs) working on an area of 56 km maximum radius from base, and calculated on 1977 telephone charge rates, is:

a.m. .. 24p.
p.m. .. 15p.

Here is an example of a job specification for a telesales operator at Ross Foods. From this you will see the kind of sophisticated activities their operators are expected to perform – and which they do, very successfully.

Job Specification for a TeleSales Operator

Job title: Telesales operator.
Department: Sales.
Responsible to: District manager.
Works in close association with: All plant and depot management, representatives and distribution managers.
Main purposes and scope of the job: To service via the telephone a predetermined number of calls and in doing so promote the sale of the company's products to reach the targets and objectives set.

Responsibilities and Duties

1 It is the telesales operator's responsibility to see that every one of his/her customers is contacted on the day as prescribed in the Kardex file according to the call-rate set.

2 As the job is based on a sales and service principle the telesales operator is expected to use his/her skills to ensure adequate stocks are held of those products and packages purchased by the customer to last between each telephone call.

3 To inform the customer at every opportunity of the products and services available from the company and in doing so endeavour to improve on the product and pack holding and volume throughput.

4 To optimize on all sales promotions when run.

5 To work in close liaison with the sales representatives with

87

the view to improving the management and development of their area.

6 Keep management informed at all times of dealer wants and needs. Furthermore to follow-up on all competitive activity.

7 To receive and act upon telephone orders that come into the plant or depot and control the buying stability of outlets under his/her control.

8 Ensure that all documents are legible and correctly made out.

9 To keep adequate records of daily activity such as calls made, buyers, non-buyers, sales by pack and product, including new packs of products introduced, so that the daily, weekly and monthly reports can be raised.

10 Ensure that all dealer record cards are updated at all times.

11 To attend sales training meetings or conferences held by local management or by the company.

In his/her capacity as a telesales operator, the employee will be responsible to management for:

(a) A quantifiable number of route customer calls.
(b) Telephone-sales communications with the trade.
(c) Customer relations within his/her section of work.
(d) Personal selling to existing customers.
(e) Sales development of his/her route calls.
(f) Clerical processing of his/her relative administration.
(g) Statistical control of his/her sales targets and performance.
(h) The recording of all relative information and sales data.
(i) The reporting of all relative information and sales data.

Descriptive detail of items listed from (a) to (i)
Route calls   As required by management to provide full cover of a normal working day in relation to specific targets.

Telephone communications   By establishing verbal communications on a regular and planned basis, with clarity, manner, knowledge and personality.

Customer relations   By establishing goodwill and credibility between the customer, himself/herself and the company by service, reliability and actioning dealer problems.

Personal selling   By direct telephone selling, with the buyer, on all his/her existing accounts.

Sales development By personal planning from information recorded on the sales record cards. Maximize sales using the full range of products and packages available, by knowledgeable presentation allied to any promotional activities currently operating with the trade.

Clerical processing By accurate utilization of all relative documentation associated with customer orders and allied paperwork.

Statistical control By regular attention to set targets and performance figures as laid down by management.

Recording By regular utilization of all relative documentation in line with his/her activities and duties on all aspects of control procedures associated with his/her employment as a telesales operator.

Reporting By his/her regular submission of all relative information in reference to the work and the customers, together with any problem associated.

M

Memos to the Troops

Anything in writing is highly dangerous, because words can be interpreted in so many different ways. Few managers ever bother about this. Worse still, many managers never send memos to their troops at all.

Regular communication between manager and salesmen is essential. Out there in the field it's a lonely job. A salesman needs to feel wanted. To be told often that he is doing a good job. It's part of motivation.

Memos come in all shapes and sizes. The simplest and most effective in motivational terms are the 'well done' kind:

Just a note to say well done on the Radford order, George.
Their purchasing team are a bunch of hard nuts to crack.
Keep up the good work.

Doubly effective because invariably the salesman's wife will read it.

Memos that bring *change* are the most dangerous kind – change in procedures, change of policy, change of prices, change in delivery schedules.

The secret for these kind of memos is to always explain *why* the change is necessary, and then to go on and explain the benefits to the company, the salesmen or whatever that will result from the change *in simple language*.

Now dig out a few of the memos you have sent out to your troops over the past weeks, and have a good nightmare.

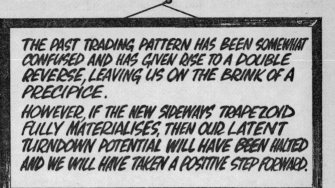

THE PAST TRADING PATTERN HAS BEEN SOMEWHAT CONFUSED AND HAS GIVEN RISE TO A DOUBLE REVERSE, LEAVING US ON THE BRINK OF A PRECIPICE.
HOWEVER, IF THE NEW SIDEWAYS TRAPEZOID FULLY MATERIALISES, THEN OUR LATENT TURNDOWN POTENTIAL WILL HAVE BEEN HALTED AND WE WILL HAVE TAKEN A POSITIVE STEP FORWARD.

Moonlighting

Moonlighters are harder to catch than leadswingers. They either use their energies in pursuing another after-hours job or, worse still, they sell someone else's products at the same time as they are selling yours, and to the same customers.

Do not ever advocate, encourage or allow any form of moonlighting. If a salesman isn't totally committed to your company, its objectives and his target, get rid of him.

I've known salesmen with their own businesses with dress shops which they run on Saturdays, with fish and chip saloons, with market stalls, who act as barmen every night of the week, who play in dance bands, who sell insurance on the side, who are part-time lecturers at technical colleges, who trade in antiques, jewellery, porn, contraceptives, instant print and who sell advertising space as well as fork-lift trucks.

There are two million known moonlighters in Britain, those who are registered with the Inland Revenue as having two jobs. On the iceberg principle, that means there may be as least sixteen million in total.

Any kind of moonlighting saps your employee's energies and *you* lose. Make sure all your salesmen are prohibited from carrying on any other kind of business activity by building an appropriate clause into their service contracts.

If you have such a clause, and you catch someone moonlighting, fire him on the spot. And make sure the rest of the team know why.

Motivation

For any kind of motivation to work, it has to relate to something that will happen in the *future*. Not the present, nor the past.

Thus it is no use paying a salesman more money in the hope that he will perform better in the months ahead. He won't, and you'll never be able to take the extra money back from him either. A month after its award, he'll firmly believe he got it by right.

There are two kinds of motivation, negative and positive. Negative is commonly referred to as 'the big stick' and uses fear as its main weapon. Positive is commonly referred to as 'the carrot' and uses pleasurable or better things to look forward to as its main tool.

The big stick doesn't work any more, except with salesmen of elderly years, who know they won't get another job if they

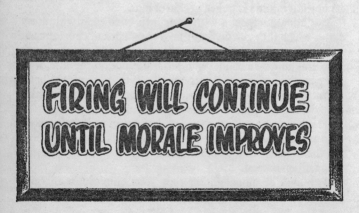

lose the one they have. With younger salesmen, they'll take only so much, then they'll tell you to what to do with the job and leave of their own accord. Motivating by fear is both futile and senseless.

For the carrot to work, in making salesmen strive for greater things, the carrot itself must be seen by all to be attainable. If it is too far out of reach, only the high-flyers will make any effort to reach it. The rest will quickly decide there is no point in trying.

Motivation is like quicksands – constantly changing. What turns one man on one year may not turn him on the next. Always be alive to this. Keep up to date. And remember, everyone is different. What motivates one salesman may not work on the others. Tailor your motivational package to each individual.

Norms

In the section on personal performance I discuss a system for measuring and monitoring each salesman's effectiveness.

If you take the quarterly totals for each of your salesmen and add them all together, you can calculate performance norms for the sales force as a whole.

Figures 14 and 15 show examples of how to produce norms and sales force totals on just two pieces of specially designed card.

The value in calculating norms for performance is:

1 Each salesman can relate his own performance, in detail, to the average (norm) performance for the sales force as a whole.
2 Where any salesman has a personal performance ratio which is worse than the norm ratio he strives during the next quarter to bring his performance at least up to the norm performance.
3 In achieving this improvement, the company norms for the next quarter are automatically better than for the last quarter.
4 The whole process then becomes *automatic*. Performance steadily improves because no one wants a ratio which is worse than the norm. You can almost sit back and let it happen.

SALESMAN	TOTAL CALLS	NO INTER-VIEWS	CALLS ON USERS	ORDERS FROM USERS	TOTAL ORDER VALUE FROM USERS	FIRST EVER CALLS	CALLS ON PROSP'TS	PROP'LS SUB-MITTED	ORDERS FROM PROSP'TS	TOTAL ORDER VALUE FROM PROSPECTS
J.Watson	205	44	203	44	13,884	46	85	33	18	4,669
R.Briggs	264	32	168	27	8,903	51	96	44	27	6,463
L.Sotton	249	28	202	31	9.275	36	47	11	8	2,761
F.White	296	31	175	27	8,740	68	121	57	31	7,892
G.Hope	321	43	212	41	8,202	59	109	49	28	6,720
A.Rolfe	199	37	142	20	7,966	29	57	19	14	7,995
B.Stein	255	42	170	26	8,449	56	85	39	22	5,977
S.Arm	253	30	166	32	9,791	66	87	48	24	6,502
J.Jones	241	21	175	31	9,464	41	66	35	20	4,744
W.Ask	302	26	204	52	13,242	64	98	52	29	8,842
TOTALS	2,268	334	1,817	331	97,976	516	851	387	221	58,565

Abortive call Ratio	$\dfrac{A\ 2668}{B\ 334}$	8.0 to 1	Average calls on a Prospect	$\dfrac{G\ 851}{F\ 516}$	1.65
			Calls to proposals Ratio (Prospects)	$\dfrac{G\ 851}{H\ 387}$	2.2 to 1
Calls to orders Ratio (Users)	$\dfrac{C\ 1817}{D\ 331}$	5.5 to 1	Proposals to orders Ratio (Prospects)	$\dfrac{H\ 387}{J\ 221}$	1.75 to 1
Average order Value (Users)	$\dfrac{E\ 97976}{D\ 331}$	£296	Average order Value (Prospects)	$\dfrac{K\ 58565}{J\ 221}$	£265

Figure 14. Example of a company performance norms card.

ACTIVITY ANALYSIS   PERIOD SECOND QUARTER   WEEKS 14 to 26

SALESMAN	0	1	2	3	4	5	6	7	8	9	A	B	C	D	E	F	G	H	J	K	TOTAL CALLS	TOTAL BY APPOINT- MENT	% of Total	TOTAL FROM LEADS	% of Total	TOTAL SERVICE CALLS	% of Total
J WATSON	23	21	33	52	12	6	30	39	81	46	51	41	37	32	14	32	17	21	13		2285	144	50	29	10	15	5·2
R BEARS	16	26	21	57	14	41	27	42	72	46	52	40	35	35	11	8	19	21	31	9	244	192	73	26	10	17	6·4
L SUTTON	16	14	31	53	10	39	26	34	49	48	84	44	33	31	10	9	26	16	31	44	249	103	41	13	5	6	2·4
F WINTERS	24	18	29	46	13	18	18	35	85	25	49	31	27	8	8	44	9	10	31	12	296	244	82	61	9	14	6·4
G HOPKINS	29	21	24	44	11	4	17	42	99	15	92	24	45	13	13	11	53	21	31	11	324	272	58	24	11	24	7·5
A ROLFE	36	57	20	42	12	17	4	41	44	14	92	81	27	4	2	41	11	9	40	12	199	140	70	44	21	4	2·0
D STEIN	19	27	25	52	9	18	22	14	95	47	105	30	22	17	10	38	17	31	25	4	255	241	59	16	11	7	2·7
S JONES	20	19	24	65	13	39	39	42	94	25	94	94	36	36	41	45	28	23	7	31	252	121	50	24	7	12	8·5
J JONES	24	21	20	44	11	20	42	12	98	69	114	92	31	12	6	7	42	32	31	42	201	901	44	244	10	8	9·2
W ASWORTH	27	31	23	49	12	21	32	21	84		112	53	44	28	7	6	44	23	81	8	205	582	46		41		
TOTALS	232	258	252	555	242	127	471	357													2,668	1854		272	101	121	1·5

Figure 15. Example of a sales force activity analysis card.

Office Costs

One of your objectives is to keep them as low as possible, just like the salesmen's expenses.

Get all your office staff to work at the checklist shown in figure 16. It doesn't just aim itself at reducing costs, it is also useful for improving office efficiency.

Organizing Sales Conferences

Most companies hold an annual sales conference. In the navy, it would probably be called the 'wash-up' after an exercise. The conference usually analyses the performance of the last sales period and then goes into plans for the next sales period. Individual members of the company get up and talk about sundry specific subjects and a couple of visiting speakers may be brought in from outside to give a fresh approach to some sales point or other.

Or the company may run an annual sales training session and use its own management to do the actual training, if it is capable. Either way, two or three days are involved and the entire sales force has to be accommodated around the venue for the duration of the festivities.

There are several important factors which contribute to a successful conference. The first is to gain the maximum amount of participation from *all* the people there. Without

	N/A	YES	NO	PAR	?	ACT
1 Do all departments conform to a uniform filing system?						
2 If no, does this lead to confusion when staff are 'on loan' from another department?						
3 .... or to any other form of delay or confusion?						
4 Is our present system simple enough to enable junior staff to rapidly retrieve files and documents?						
5 Are our filing procedures formalised and in writing for the benefit of new management and staff?						
6 Do we have over-duplication of information? — copies or documents which are filed and never again referred to.						
7 Do we have under-duplication of information? — constant requests between departments for files and documents.						
8 Do we have rigid accountability on all photocopying?						
9 .... and do we occasionally check that copies in excess of requirements are not being produced?						
10 Are telephone switchboard procedures in writing?						
11 Do we fully appreciate the importance of efficient switchboard operation?						
12 .... and the need to maintain this particular 'company image' at the highest possible level?						
13 Is the switchboard operator advised daily upon those executives who are away?						
14 .... and also advised upon those who will be absent for several hours?						
15 Do secretaries/typists frequently await incoming mail to be processed before they can commence work?						

16 Does the sorting and distribution of mail receive priority every morning?

17 .... and subsequent mail likewise?

18 If no, does this result in operational delays and/or executives and their secretaries working overtime in order to process the mail?

19 Do any executives/managers have semi-idle secretaries because they regularly delay processing their correspondence?

20 If yes, could staff reductions be made if they processed more promptly?

21 ... or conversely, could staff be made available to them in the latter part of the day? .... and thus reduce staff.

22 .... or if dictation equipment were to be installed?

23 Have we assessed the level of activity at which we should review/introduce dictation equipment?

24 If it became necessary, for financial reasons, for staff to be reduced by 20% do we know *now* how these reductions would be effected?

25 Could any such reduction be made now — without serious loss of efficiency?

26 If yes, have we prepared recommendations to this effect and submitted them to senior management?

27 Are workloads reasonably and evenly distributed among female staff?

28 In order to minimise typing have we analysed our correspondence within the last twelve months with a view to standardisation of replies that are in common and repetitive use?

29 Have our present standard letters been reviewed within the last 12 months?

Figure 16. An office activity checklist.

this, the ultimate objective will never be attained – that everyone should go away from the conference totally committed to the plans discussed and firmly believing that they are right.

Conferences should not be used as an opportunity for management to lean heavily on the sales force, and any form of oppression should be avoided. Oppression can come in various forms. Enclosed by just the four walls of his head office, a salesman can feel intimidated by his surroundings, switch to the defensive and shut up like a clam for the entire proceedings. This varies with the company, of course, but the first general rule for running conferences is:

Avoid Having Them on Company Premises

Apart from the reason just expounded, few companies have the right facilities for a successful conference. The time wasted shuttling back and forth for meals at a nearby hotel and sorting out accommodation in similar adjacent abodes, usually costs as much as if the company had put the entire thing into the right sort of hotel in the first place. Which brings us to our second general rule.

Select the Right Sort of Hotel

Of course, cost is an important factor, but the cost difference between a good and a bad hotel is insignificant when compared with the value of increased business which the company wants the conference to launch. A bad hotel can ruin a whole year's motivation and performance.

The right sort of hotel should have the following facilities:

1 Single bedrooms with their own bathrooms. (Make the sales force look forward to the event.)
2 A really good restaurant. (Remember, the way to a man's heart is through his stomach – it's true for salesmen, too).
3 Really comfortable chairs in the conference room. (The mind can only absorb as much as the behind can endure.)

4 The right shaped conference room. (And large enough. Plenty of air. If in doubt, always double the size. More about the right shape later, under 'room layout'.)

5 Good visual aids. (That means blackboards, flip charts, cine screens, projectors, effective blackout, good lighting, microphones, etc.)

6 A staff that knows about the conference business. (Nothing can break a conference organizer's heart quicker than having a hotel staff that hasn't a clue what a good conference needs.)

7 Adequate car parking.

8 Silence. (Never pick a hotel on a main trunk road, or in the centre of a town. If in doubt, stay for a night yourself and see.)

One point when booking reservations for a conference – never rely on the telephone alone. Go and see for yourself. I only made this mistake once, in London. Never again will I rely on a hotel manager's verbal interpretation. It wasn't really the manager's fault. I failed to convey to him what I was looking for. It's so easily done, especially when time is short.

And so on to the third general rule.

Get the Room Layout Right

There is a hotel in the Midlands that has recently spent nearly £100,000 on a new conference wing. I will never use it. Whoever designed the new wing obviously had no idea of how a good conference should be run.

The 'sharp end' of the room, where the speaker has to stand, has superb picture windows. Did you ever try to concentrate on a speaker on a summer afternoon when he's standing in front of dazzling sunlight? The strain is tremendous. The audience cannot see a thing. Again, the entrances to the conference room are close to the picture windows. So anyone creeping in and out can be seen by the entire audience. Another concentration sapper. It may sound petty to you, but it really is very important.

For a really effective conference – or training session – the audience should face a blank wall. Windows should preferably be behind the audience, so that the delegates aren't tempted to glance out when a pretty girl passes by. The only objects in front of that blank wall should be the visual aids being used. The blackboard, the flip chart, the cine screen. Entrances should always, but always, be at the back of the room. As conference organizer yourself, you will be in and out all the time, sorting out minor details.

Always provide your delegates with tables. I have seen so many conferences where the delegates sat theatre style for three whole days. Nowhere to write notes, nowhere to lean elbows and ease the aching behind. Disaster. The optimum

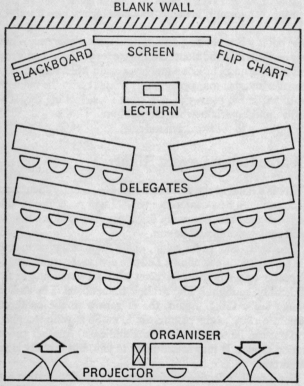

Figure 17.

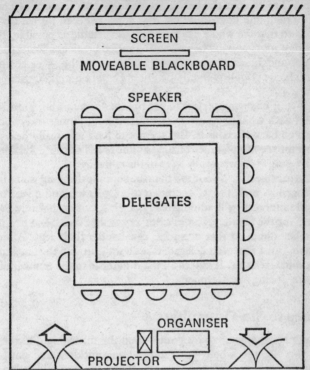

Figure 18.

layout of tables and chairs is as shown in figure 17. Nobody in the room has to angle his head or body more than forty-five degrees either way to see everything going on at the front.

The square layout, figure 18, is sometimes preferred. It is satisfactory for a group discussion, where everyone around the square is participating, but if there are speakers using one end, especially ones who like walking a lot, as I do, it only takes half an hour for some of the delegates to get cricks in their necks.

Allow at least three feet of table per man, and make sure there is always adequate fresh water available for all.

Now a few words about the format of the actual conference itself. Try to split the entire proceedings into sessions of not more than one hour duration. Use films between formal sessions so that the whole day's work is as versatile as possible. If the day starts at 0900 hours, have a coffee break at about 1100 hours and lunch at about 1300 hours. A tea break at about 1600 hours then leaves only two hours before normal finishing time.

If your company prefers to use the evenings as well, a sentiment with which I heartily concur, break for dinner early and then go back afterwards. But try not to have any really heavy stuff for the after-dinner business. The levels of concentration will be only half what they were in the morning.

As organizer, it is your job to make sure the drinking water is changed at each break, 0900, 1100, 1300, 1500 and 1830. A good hotel staff will automatically do this, but do not rely on them for the first day, just in case. Try to take coffee and tea in another room, so that everyone can stretch their legs. After lunch, insist that each delegate takes a walk around the hotel to get some fresh air. It makes all the difference to the number of yawns during the afternoon.

Keep to the Timetable

Don't allow anyone to overrun – even the managing director. If you do, the whole proceedings can quickly come down round your ears. And while we are talking about the timetable, and your months of planning before the actual conference – because that's how long it takes – remember that most good hotels are taking bookings up to two years in advance, so don't leave everything until the last minute.

Films need three months booking notice to make absolutely sure of getting them on the right day. Rank Film Library, PO Box 70, Great West Road, Brentford, Middlesex (telephone 01-968 9222), and Video Arts Ltd, Dumbarton House, 68 Oxford Street, London WIN 9LA (01-637 7288), and Guild Sound & Vision Ltd, Woodston House, Oundle Road, Peterborough PE2 9PZ (0733 63122), are the main sources of supply. Or Structured Training Ltd if you want a presenter as well.

Regional Sales Meetings

Many companies have regional managers whose job it is to train and motivate the salesmen under their command. To do this, regional managers hold meetings once a month, or once a quarter.

The same rules we have discussed for sales conferences also apply to these smaller meetings. Except, of course, there is no accommodation requirement. But a professional outlook on such a meeting by the regional manager can work wonders in motivation. I've also seen exactly the opposite – a half-day jolly in a grotty little room with no heating – which had such a demoralizing effect on the salesmen that the regional manager was openly held in derision by his men.

Personal Performance

Most sales managers would say that measuring and monitoring a salesman's performance or effectiveness is one of the most difficult and most elusive things to get your teeth into.

Not so. It's the way they try to measure and monitor which makes the job difficult. Done properly, monitoring personal performance is one of the easiest jobs the sales manager has to do, and one of the least time consuming.

I've spent about ten years developing systems for sales force control, and in this section I'm going to discuss what I consider is the best – SCRS, marketed by Sales Control and Record Systems Ltd. Other parts of the SCRS system are mentioned in the sections entitled Norms, Forecasting, Customer Records and If in Doubt – Ask.

Basic Principle

A sales force control, measuring or monitoring system *must* use numbers, *not* words.

All you can do with words is read them. You can't add them up, multiply them, divide them, cumulate them or anything. So all you get with words is an instant picture of today or yesterday. No sales manager has a computer for a mind, so he cannot correlate all the words he receives from his salesmen and put together an ongoing picture. He'd go mad if he tried.

You cannot judge the performance of a salesman solely on the turnover he produces in a given period of time, or the number of calls he makes each week. Personal performance measurement needs to cover much more. Here's the most effective way of doing the job properly.

Each week, every salesman submits to you a list of *all* the face-to-face calls he has made during the week, and what happened on each call. This list does *not* include telephone calls.

This weekly list is in the form shown in figure 19 and is entitled 'call analysis'. The design of the form reduces writing to a minimum. Each call takes up one line, most of the 'what happened' data being recorded as ticks. The sections covering 'industry category' and 'product groups discussed' use a master code devised by the company and common to all the salesmen. Our example shows the calls salesman J. Watson made during week 14 of the year in question. He travelled 245 miles to make the calls, and (bottom left) succeeded in submitting two proposals on prospects (not to be confused with existing customers) during the week.

You will receive one of these forms from each of your salesmen in each Monday's post along with expense claims and call plans for the next week. All you do with the information is enter the totals on two master cards you keep for each salesman. The work of entering the totals on these cards each Monday takes a few minutes only. In fact, your secretary should do it.

Figures 20 and 21 show the two master cards for salesman J. Watson. Following the numbers through from our example of his week 14 call analysis form you will see where the totals are entered in the week 14 lines on these two cards.

Four items of information must be supplied each week from headquarters (usually accounts) to complete each salesman's cards. These items are the total orders received from existing customers during the week from each salesman's territory and the total value of these orders, and likewise for prospects.

The two master cards are designed to calculate performance on a quarterly basis, which has been found by far the most suitable period, being long enough to iron out any abnormalities in the numbers due to holidays or illness and short enough to give the company time to sort out any major prob-

CALL ANALYSIS

WEEK __14__ SALESMAN __J. WATSON__

IF A CALL RESULTS IN "NO INTERVIEW" STILL TICK THE COLUMNS WHICH INDICATE WHAT KIND OF CALL IT SHOULD HAVE BEEN DATE COMPANY	Industry Category	No Interview	Call on Existing Customers	Call on Prospect (Pot. New Cust.)	First Ever Call	Follow up of Lead
M PRESS STEEL	A		✓			
" POTTERSBY & CO	B	✓		✓	✓	
" J.E.B ENGINEERS	A		✓			
" HEREFORD & CO	D		✓			
" EATON & CO	C		✓			
T WYMAN WELDING	B		✓			
" I.B.E.	D			✓	✓	
" SMITH DAVIDSON	B	✓		✓	✓	
" FISHER & WADE	A			✓		✓
" AUTOLIFT	B		✓			
" VICTORIA FORGE	A			✓	✓	
" ASH & CO	A	✓	✓			
" BLOGGS & SMALL	D		✓			
" EXHAUST TOOLS	B		✓			
W JONES & PLATT	G		✓			
" BEEDON SMITH	A		✓			
" DROP FORGES	B		✓			
" F. LACEY & CO	G			✓	✓	✓
" ARUNDEL DEVELOPMENT	D			✓	✓	
F C.K. VALVES	A	✓	✓			
" BRITISH STEEL	K		✓			✓
" AQUASCUTUM	U			✓		
" WAKEFIELDS	C		✓			
TOTALS		4	15	8	5	3

NUMBER OF PROPOSALS
SUBMITTED ON PROSPECTS
(POT. NEW CUSTOMERS)   __2__
DURING WEEK

A	B	C	D	E
8	6	2	5	0

Figure 19. Example of a salesman's call analysis form.

Appointment	Proposal Requested	Action Request	Order Secured	Service Call	0	1	2	3	4	5	6	7	8	9
✓	▓		▓											✓
													✓	
✓		✓	✓									✓		
						✓	✓							
					✓									
													✓	
✓	✓	✓						✓						
							✓						✓	
													✓	
									✓		✓			✓
✓													✓	
✓	✓	✓	✓					✓						
✓					✓									
✓		✓					✓						✓	
✓													✓	
	✓	✓						✓						
											✓	✓		
		✓						✓						
	✓						✓				✓			
7	3	5	4	0	2	1	4	4	1	0	3	2	7	2
					0	1	2	3	4	5	6	7	8	9

F	G	H	J	K	INDUSTRY CATEGORY TOTALS	BUSINESS MILEAGE
0	2	0	1	2		245

PERSONAL PERFORMANCE RECORD

SECOND QUARTER YEAR 1977 SALESMAN J. WATSON

WEEK	MILEAGE	OVERALL MILES PER CALL RATIO. CUMULATIVES	TOTAL CALLS	ABORTIVE CALL RATIO. CUMULATIVES	NO INTERVIEW	TOTAL CALLS ON USERS	EXISTING CUSTOMERS CALLS TO ORDER RATIO. CUMULATIVES	TOTAL ORDER RCD FROM USERS	AVERAGE ORDER VALUE REPEAT BUSINESS. CUMULATIVES	TOTAL ORDER VALUE FROM USERS
14	245		26		4	18		4		824
15	240		24		5	16		3		716
16	235		25		2	14		5		1016
17	168		20		6	14		1		168
18	196		24		4	17		4		1870
19	247		26		1	15		0		0
20	189		16		3	12		4		1250
21	304		26		5	18		5		1680
22	202		24		4	20		2		420
23	98		10		3	10		0		0
24	240		26		1	19		6		3190
25	175		20		1	15		6		1900
26	166	2660 288	21	288 44	5	15	203 44	4	13,884 44	880
COMPANY NORM		9.2		6.5 / 8.0			4.6 / 5.5		315 / 296	

PROSPECTS

WEEK	FIRST EVER CALLS	AVERAGE CALLS ON A PROSPECT CUMULATIVES	TOTAL CALLS ON PROS.	CALLS TO PROPOSALS RATIO CUMULATIVES	PROPOSALS SUBMITTED	PROPOSALS TO ORDER RATIO CUMULATIVES	TOTAL ORDERS RCD FROM PROSPECTS	AVERAGE ORDER VALUE NEW BUSINESS CUMULATIVES	TOTAL ORDER VALUE FROM PROSPECTS
14	5		8		2		1		680
15	3		8		3		2		420
16	6		11		1		3		1120
17	6		6		4		2		468
18	4		7		2		0		0
19	2		11		3		2		378
20	2		4		4		1		185
21	5		8		5		2		410
22	4		4		1		0		0
23	0		0		0		0		0
24	3		7		4		3		526
25	4		6		2		1		286
26	2	46 / 86	6	86 / 33	2	33 / 18	1	18 / 4669	196
		RATIO Z 1·8		RATIO X 2·6		RATIO Y 1·8		259	
		COMPANY NORM 1·65		COMPANY NORM 2·2		COMPANY NORM 1·75		COMPANY NORM 269	

SECOND QUARTER'S REPEAT BUSINESS TARGET	
10,500	
—	1st QUARTER DEFICIT

SECOND QUARTER'S NEW BUSINESS TARGET	
5,750	
1,205	1st QUARTER DEFICIT

Figure 20. Example of a salesman's personal performance record card.

SALES ANALYSIS
SECOND QUARTER

YEAR 1977   SALESMAN J. WATSON

PRODUCT GROUP ANALYSIS

WEEK	0	+	1	+	2	+	3	+	4	+	5	+	6	+	7	+	8	+	9	+
14	2		1		4		5		1				3		2		7		2	
15	1		4		3		6						2		1		4		3	
16	3		1		4		7		1		1		3		3		8		4	
17	1		1		2		3						1		1		6		3	
18	2		2		2		2		1				3		3		8		2	
19	3		4		4		5		2		1		3		3		7		5	
20	2		1		3		3		1		1		2		4		7		4	
21	1				1		5		2				3		3		6		5	
22	1		2		3		4		1				2		4		7		6	
23					1		2						1		2		3		1	
24	4		3		3		6		2		2		4		4		6		4	
25	2		1		2		3		1		1		2		3		5		3	
26	1		2		1		2						1		3		7		5	
TOTALS	23		22		33		53		12		6		30		36		81		46	

CUSTOMER CATEGORY ANALYSIS

WEEK	A	B	C	D	E	F	G	H	J	K
14	8	6	2	5			2		1	2
15	6	4	3	2	1	2	4		1	1
16	5	3	4	2	2	3	3	1	1	1
17	3	2	4	3	1	1	4		2	
18	4	4	2	4	2	2	4		2	
19	6	3	4	1	1	1	4	1	3	2
20		4	3			2	3	2		2
21	4	5	2	3	1	3	2	3	2	2
22	3	4	3	2	2		2	3	5	
23	1	1	2		1		1		3	1
24	7	3	2	4	1	1	2	2	4	
25	1	2	4	3			3	2	5	
26	3	2	2	4	2	1	3	2	2	1
	51	41	37	33	14	14	37	17	31	

CALLS ANALYSIS

WEEK	TOTAL CALLS	BY APP'T	FROM LEAD	SERVICE CALLS
14	26	11	3	0
15	24	19	2	1
16	25	14	4	0
17	20	10	3	3
18	24	6	2	0
19	26	13	2	5
20	16	12	1	0
21	26	9	4	0
22	24	11	3	1
23	10	4	0	4
24	26	16	1	0
25	20	10	3	0
26	21	9	1	1
TOTALS	288	144	29	15

Figure 21. Example of a salesman's sales analysis card.

lems the numbers pinpoint before these problems get out of hand.

Apart from entering the numbers on these cards each Monday, there is no further action necessary until the end of the thirteen-week period, in our case, after the end of week 26. Then you or your secretary total all the columns and by dividing the smaller totals into the larger for each pair of numbers on the personal performance record card, figure 20, you calculate each salesman's performance for that quarter in respect of *eight* different aspects of his job.

From the totals on the sales analysis master card, figure 21, you pinpoint any part of the product range that salesman might be neglecting, and likewise for any industry important to the company. The bottom right columns totals give you information on how effective each salesman is at making appointments, how effective your sales promotion and advertising activities have been in each territory and how much time each salesman has been forced to spend on non-selling activities.

All the data you need, on two A4 size cards, to pinpoint specific problems and implement remedial action without delay.

By comparing one quarter's figures with another, a pattern of personal performance can clearly be established. The ratios are also extremely valuable in calculating accurate and attainable sales targets for each salesman, but this we have dealt with under Forecasting.

To find out what else can be done with these cards, read the section on Norms.

Post-Mortems

Always find out in detail why an important piece of business the company was chasing was lost. Get everyone together and hold a post-mortem. You need to pinpoint all the reasons you lost the order, so that everyone can make sure the same mistakes don't get made again.

But make sure your post-mortems don't develop into hatchet meetings or recrimination sessions. If they do, you'll never find out what went wrong.

Priorities

Always get your priorities in the right order.

Start each week by getting together with your secretary and listing the things that *must* be done that week. Then list the things that *should* be done. Then list the things that *could* be done, given the time.

Never get your *musts*, *shoulds* and *coulds* mixed up. And always make sure everyone in your department knows what's on the list, except for any confidential matters, of course. This way, your staff will *help* you complete the list, rather than hinder.

Figure 22 shows an example of a daily job priority form, used for sales promotional purposes by a printing group.

Musts for Today

Date

Northbourne Press Limited
Letterpress and Lithographic Printers
North Street, Coventry CV2 3PF
Telephone (0203) 453711
Member of The Courier Press Group

URGENT   DONE

☐ _____ ☐

☐ _____ ☐

☐ _____ ☐

☐ _____ ☐

☐ _____ ☐

☐ _____ ☐

☐ _____ ☐

☐ _____ ☐

☐ _____ ☐

☐ _____ ☐

☐ _____ ☐

☐ _____ ☐

☑ *Phone Northbourne* _____ ☐

Figure 22. Example of a daily job priority form.

Quotations and Proposals

Only if you are selling at the lowest price and with the shortest delivery will you get away with using the traditional British quotation, full of Victoriana ('thank you for your esteemed . . .') technical specification, terms of payment, ex-works price and with all your terms and conditions for doing business in pale grey 6pt type on the back.

If you haven't got the lowest price or the shortest delivery, you will be losing most of the business that you quote for. Change the rules. Change the way you quote and start submitting decent selling proposals.

I cannot do better, in explaining how and why, than to reproduce an article I wrote for the Institute of Purchasing Management.

Don't Accept the Lowest Bid

Every buyer has to suffer from time to time from the traditional task of collecting quotations from selected suppliers for a particular requirement and – having received the quotations – try to analyse the gobbledy-gook and decide which of the offers gives him the best all-round deal.

No longer is price the only consideration, of course. Quality, performance, maintenance costs, delivery and reliability are all factors which will influence the final decision one way or the other.

But it does often seem to be far too difficult for the buyer to establish which of, say, three or four quotations is really the best bet. Suppliers are so loath to provide information in their quotations which is going to make the job easier.

Here's a good example:

Dear Sirs,
We beg to thank you for your esteemed inquiry, and have pleasure in quoting as follows, subject to the terms and conditions stated on the back hereof:

> Four lanes of Bloggs Proximity Dual Duty Overhead Conveyors Kx 500/4.
> Loading 500 kg per trolley.
> Speed 20 metres per minute.
> Automatic electronic beam safety equipment fitted every 6 metre run.
> All basically in accordance with customer drawing 2B/42/764.
> *For the sum of £14,764.50 Ex works.*
> Delivery 18/22 weeks from confirmation of official customer order.
> Terms of payment: Net cash 30 days.
> Prices hold good for 60 days only from date of this quotation.

We trust that the above quotation will prove to be satisfactory, and we look forward to the receipt of your esteemed order in due course when it will receive our most careful attention.
Yours faithfully,
Per Pro Bloggs Handling Ltd
E & O E

Every time I see a quotation like that it makes me sigh heavily and gives me indigestion for a week. Do suppliers honestly think they can still get business with this kind of drivel? Do they ever stop to think what the poor old buyer is up against on the receiving end?

Specification – price – delivery. Just that and nothing more. Specification – price – delivery. Not even any attempt to explain what the hell a Bloggs Proximity Dual Duty Overhead Conveyor is – or what it does. Okay, the salesman told you a month ago, and the leaflet is lying around somewhere, but do they really expect you to remember all that technical jargon the salesman explained to you four or five weeks back? Mad if they do. What proportion of your total time has this job they're quoting for taken up these last four weeks. Five per cent? Two per cent? Let's see them remember much of a discussion a month past when ninety-eight per cent of their time has been taken up with other problems and requirements, most of them just as important, or more so.

So there is the buyer, sitting at his desk, looking at three or four typical British quotations. Specification – price – delivery. Specification – price – delivery. Hey, this one doesn't even give a spec. It's just a list of equipment with prices, totalled at the bottom.

Which offer does he decide to accept?

If we assume that delivery is not a critical factor in the particular case we are examining, or alternatively all the quotations offer an acceptable delivery, the entire decision-making exercise hangs on the specification and the price.

So specifications are examined closely. The snag is that there is so little meaningful information. All the buyer – or his engineer – can do is establish whether or not the equipment offered will meet the criteria laid down – whether it will, in fact, do the job the company wants done. Not how *well* it will do the job. Not how much *better* it will do the job than the criteria laid down. Not how it will do the job in a different and more efficient way than the company stipulated.

Just that it will do the job that has to be done. A minimum specification requirement if you like. A British standard pass mark.

There is our poor buyer, faced with three or four British standard passes – all of which will satisfy the minimum requirements – but none of which tell him how much *better* they are, whether they qualify for a 'credit' or a 'distinction', rather than a pass.

So like many an examiner in academic circles, our buyer wields his rubber stamp *pass* on all the quotations.

Delivery dealt with.

Specification dealt with.

That only leaves price – and faced with this particular set of circumstances, only a fool would order anything but the cheapest. The quotation offering the lowest price *should* get the order, and most times does.

But has the buyer made sure his company has the best deal? I say *no*.

Not his fault entirely. To make really sure, he needs to examine very closely indeed each piece of equipment offered, compare specifications, translate the specifications into figures or facts meaningful to him and his company's requirement, project those facts and figures over a period of time to establish overall gains, savings, maintenance costs, etc., allow for labour, cost of finance, sales forecasts for established production – and so on – to arrive at a true comparison of offer to offer.

Only then can he turn to price and decide which one to buy. And only then will he be able to use his comparison calculations to prove that, despite a price £1,000 higher than the offer from *A*, offer *B* gives a better overall deal, and the extra price paid will be recouped in maintenance savings, less scrap, higher output, reduced labour or whatever, inside the first six months.

So *B* gets the order. But can the buyer really be expected to go to all that trouble? Shouldn't it be the supplier's job to demonstrate how good the equipment offered is for the buyer's company?

If *you* think, as I do, that providing this all-important information is the supplier's job, here is a plan for getting *your* future suppliers to do *their* job properly – and save you a whole lot of effort and grief.

In a very much simplified form, give the suppliers some clear-cut instructions on how to tender for your business. Not specially laid out tender forms, as local authorities use, but just a single sheet of instructions – for example:

To: All suppliers.
From: J. E. Fenton, Chief Buyer.
Subject: Procedure for submitting quotations.

All quotations to this company should give the information as below and in the chronological order as below. Quotations which do not follow this procedure will not be considered.
1 Begin all quotations with a brief statement of the objectives we wish to achieve by having your equipment/products/services.
2 Follow this statement of objectives with a brief outline of your

recommendations, and explain – briefly – how your recommendations fulfil our objectives.

3 Elaborate on item 2 with a list of any additional benefits we will receive from your recommendations, other than the information given under item 2.

4 Explain, with the full use of figures, finance, times, labour rates, maintenance costs, depreciation periods, production outputs, whichever are relevant, how we can justify the purchase of the equipment/products/services. All prices must be inclusive, i.e. include delivery, installation, commissioning or whatever necessary.

5 State the guarantee you provide, give details of your aftersales service organization and how it operates, and add at least three third party references that we can contact, i.e. firms using similar equipment/products/services and in our area.

Finally, don't write your quotation in 'Victoriana' ('thank you for your esteemed inquiry'; 'look forward to the favour of', etc.), write it in plain, modern English.

The result of such a set of instructions could be something like this. Remember the Bloggs Proximity Dual Duty Overhead Conveyor? Well the, opening section of the 'new look' quotation might now read:

As we understand it, you require:

(a) A fully automatic means of transporting up to 600 car bodies an hour across the roads which separate your No. 1 and No. 2 assembly shops.

(b) A built-in safety system which will instantly stop the above transportation in the event of the body units becoming dislodged.

(c) Installation of the system so as to cause minimum disruption of your production flow.

Quite a bit more meaningful, don't you think? Here's another example of opening objectives:

We agreed at our last discussion that you wanted to achieve the following:

(a) Provide mechanized handling facilities to enable up to 2,000 tonnes of fragile cargo to be offloaded from ship to shore during one normal working shift.

(b) Extend these facilities by the end of the first year's operation so as to completely turn round a 10,000/15,000 tonne cargo vessel in 36 hours.

(c) Provide full taining for your staff in the operation and maintenance of the equipment needed for these facilities.

These kind of opening sections set the scene for the rest of the quotation.

The most important section for any buyer in this new style quotation is *financial justification*. This is the information which really makes it easy for you to compare a number of offers and pinpoint the true best. This is where the supplier tells you what you are getting for your money.

Example 1

Your existing handling plant effects a throughput of 100 units per hour, on a 24 hour basis.

The proposed new system will increase this throughput to 150 units per hour.

This gives you an increase in production, in terms of units throughput, of 3,600 units per day, or 1,315,000 units per year, or 6,560,000 units in the 5 year period over which you would depreciate the plant.

Example 2

If you install this equipment, the labour force necessary for the handling operations can be reduced by 4.

Estimating a warehouseman's costs to your company at £60 per week, this would represent a saving on labour costs alone of £240 per week or £12,480 in the first year.

On an initial capital investment of £14,764.50, the cost will be recovered from these labour savings in

$$\frac{14,754.50}{12,480} = 1.183 \text{ years}$$

Over your normal 5 year depreciation period for this type of plant, and assuming a labour cost increase of 10 per cent per year, your net savings would be as follows:

1st year labour saving	£12,480.00
2nd year labour saving	£13,728.00
3rd year labour saving	£15,100.80
4th year labour saving	£16,610.88
5th year labour saving	£18,271.97
	£76,191.65
less cost of equipment	£14,764.50
Net saving	£61,427.15

(I am tempted to add at this point that if you have the task of justifying any purchase of capital equipment to your own board of directors, these are the kind of figures that will make that job very easy. And if those pessimists at the top *still* say the company can't afford it, there is another arrow still to be fired.)

Example 3

If you were to lease this equipment over 5 years, the cost of the rentals each week, on a capital price of £14,764.50 would be £75.67 per week.

This applies to non-development grant areas. If the equipment is used in a 22 per cent grant area, the rentals would be only £50.72 per week.

Your labour savings amount to £240 per week in the first year, more in subsequent years. Thus, if you lease the equipment, it won't cost one penny and will still save you upwards of £190 per week.

Example 4

Financial justification can be set out for products like pumps, valves, fluorescent lightfittings, electronic components, as well as for production equipment.

Let's take a ball valve. A particularly fine valve. Better than anything else on the market. For one specific size, the cost of the valve is £18.

But when this ball valve was introduced, the market had been buying ball valves to do the jobs this new valve was designed to do at a price of £3.

Imagine the reception given by any buyer to a specification – price – delivery quotation for this new valve.

'Six times the price? You must be joking!'

So back to the financial justification. The key benefit of the new valve was its lack of the need for maintenance. Packings had to be replaced only once a year, and even then, could be done very quickly. The old £3 valves lasted only two months before the packings needed replacement, and it was such a messy job that the works engineers usually threw the whole valve away and installed a new one.

On this basis, the following comparison costing was put together by the £18 valve suppliers:

Maintenance costs per year per valve

	New valve	*Old valve*
Initial cost of valve	£18	£3
Packing replacements required	1	6
Time allowed for replacement	20 minutes	2 hours
Therefore total replacement time/year	20 minutes	12 hours
Packing costs	£2	—
Replacement valve costs	—	£18 (6 × £3)
Works engineers' labour costs based on £3 per hour	£1	£36
Total costs per year per valve	£21	£57

These calculations do not attempt to calculate the cost of 12 hours' production per year while the valves are being replaced. This cost should be added to the £57, and likewise, the cost of 20 minutes lost production should be added to the £21.

See how much more effective those quotations could be? And how much easier it would be for you to make the *right* decision every time.

Draft a set of quotation instructions for your own business. Insist on suppliers adhering to them. Try it out on just a few for a start if you like. It's the best way of avoiding that trap we started with – being tempted to accept the lowest bid.

If your salesmen are selling lumps of machinery or any other kind of capital equipment, there is much more that they can, and should, do to back up the financial justification for the purchase in their proposals.

Here is another article I wrote for the Institute of Purchasing Management on the subject of PAYE, which explains some of the things you can get done.

PAYE – Let's have it working for us

A technique for persuading a reluctant factory owner that he really can afford that new plant.

When we are talking about capital equipment, PAYE still means 'pay-as-you-earn', but the tax man is left out in the cold.

PAYE to a factory owner means buying that much needed new production or handling or process plant, without having to save up umpteen thousands of after-tax profits, or without having to worry the bank yet again. In other words, buying the new equipment over 3 or 5 years, so that it is, in effect, earning more money than it actually costs.

Of course, there is an initial deposit to find, plus the VAT element. But the VAT can be claimed back within a month or two.

The following is going to take readers over the jumps of selling a hire-purchase deal along with a lump of new production equipment. The examples used are fictitious, but will probably fit a large number of selling situations.

Snooks Engineering Ltd needed a numerically controlled lathe to cope with a range of pipe flanges on a long-running offshore contract. Snooks were currently operating half a dozen capstan lathes to tackle this job, and their investigations, stimulated by the sales engineers from the NC lathe supplier, had shown that one NC lathe would handle the entire work being done on the six capstans, and need only one good setter/operator.

But Snooks could not raise the £50,000 needed to buy the NC lathe. The company was profitable, but not that profitable. It had assets, but not enough to negotiate a bank overdraft of that size.

So, with the help of the sales engineer, who had been trained to sell finance facilities as well as machine tools, the company looked closely at the question of buying the new lathe over 3 or 5 years. The calculations looked like this:

Cash price of NC lathe		£50,000.00
VAT at 15%		£ 7,500.00
Total cost		£57,500.00
Initial deposit of 10% plus the VAT element		£12,500.00
60 monthly payments of		£ 1,106.25
One final payment, purchase fee		£ 2.00
Then the company worked out the *net* cost:		
Total gross payments		£78,877.00
From which should be deducted:		
The VAT element	£ 7,500.00	
Regional development grant (20% in this case)	£10,000.00	
Corporation tax relief:		
(*a*) 100% first year allowance	£26,000.00	
(*b*) Allowance on interest over the 5 years	£11,115.00	
Total deductions	£54,615.00	£54,615.00
Thus, the *net* cost of the lathe was		£24,262.00

Having progressed this far, Snooks Engineering then looked closely at the savings they would make in changing over to the one NC lathe.

Five male operators would no longer be required for the job in question, and could therefore be made redundant (unions permitting) or found other, more profitable, duties. The present setter-operator, who looked after all six capstans, would be an ideal man to train in NC techniques.

Snooks took the five-year payment period as the expected useful life of the new lathe, for calculation purposes. They assumed that wages would increase by 10 per cent per year, and thus calculated the cost of the five unnecessary operators over the five years.

First year each man costs £120 per week	£31,200
Second year each man costs £132 per week	£34,320
Third year each man costs £146 per week	£37,960
Fourth year each man costs £160 per week	£41,600
Fifth year each man costs £176 per week	£45,760
Total labour costs saved	£190,840

Snooks also calculated additional savings on the changeover from having additional storage and manoeuvring space to utilize because of the removal of the six capstans, being replaced by one new machine.

Over the five years, the estimate on space utilization savings was	£4,500
Last, savings on electricity, air, lubricants, cutting fluids, swarf clearance, and maintenance were estimated, less similar costs for the new NC lathe	£3,600
Thus the total saving over five years was	£198,940
From this figure was deducted the cost of training the setter-operator in NC techniques, and redundancy payments due to the five operators no longer required	£3,200
... giving *net* gain on the whole project of	£171,478

Needless to say, Snooks Engineering didn't stop there. The ultimate sale of the second-hand capstans brought in £7,000

(£2,000 more than the initial deposit on the new lathe).

The additional profit was used to buy more production plant – faster, more economical, automatic, whatever fitted the optimum requirement – and wherever the company could show *earnings* that were more than the *payments* for the relevant plant.

As a result, Snooks has one of the most efficient, best-equipped production units in the world, and a labour force that is small, well paid and satisfied with its lot. Snooks has reequipped so swiftly that, using the benefit of the 100 per cent first year write-down allowance, the company hasn't yet had much of a corporation tax bill to pay.

But What if There are No Profits?

Our example was for a profitable company at the time the decision to buy the NC lathe was made. Yet many companies seeking to reequip may not be currently making profits. What can these companies do?

Of course, the finance house making the advance will have the last word on whether a particular company is acceptable or not, but generally a decent set of accounts over the last few years, which show stability and a certain amount of growth, will satisfy the finance house that the risks are worth taking.

Credibility is all important. Good management, forward thinking and a reasonable market for the product should all be demonstrated.

Once accepted, a company in a loss situation can gain the same financial savings as a profitable company; 100 per cent write-down allowance can still be claimed. The return will not be immediate, but will be gained when the company eventually starts making a profit.

If, like Snooks Engineering, the company qualifies for a 20 per cent or 22 per cent development grant, this grant can be claimed and the money received by the company long before its payments for the new plant reach the amount of the grant. And the company still effects the same production and labour savings. These are the things that can turn a loss-making company into a highly profitable company in a very short time.

All that is required is confidence – the confidence to make the decision to invest in new equipment *now* – and to prove those paper calculations in actual practice.

What of the Sales Engineer?

Every sales engineer who sells capital equipment needs to be conversant with the financial benefits for a company planning to invest in new plant. He needs to be armed to negotiate a sale on hire purchase, or able to call in a finance house to help him when necessary.

Many customer companies negotiate their own hire purchase deals, of course. But this is no reason for the sales engineer to neglect to lead the customer in this direction. The benefits to the sales engineer's company are very real:

1 The customer pays the deposit promptly.
2 The finance house pays the supplier promptly.

So, no cash flow problem, or extended credit taken. No bad feelings – everyone makes a fair profit.

PAYE . . . it has to make sense.

Finally, if you are still doubtful about the true effectiveness of this kind of proposal technique, talk to someone from Addressograph–Multigraph Ltd, at Hemel Hempstead, Herts.

A–M have used this technique for twenty years, for addressing equipment and for offset printing machinery. Their conversion ratio of proposals submitted to orders secured is around 2 to 1.

Recruiting Salesmen

Whether you recruit a clerk or a managing director, the national average for employees recruited who are acceptable and successful in their new job after one year is only 50 per cent.

So don't go overboard on sophisticated psychological recruitment techniques or personal recriminations. Here are a few rules to follow when recruiting salesmen.

1 Be very hard-nosed about anyone who is willing to move to you for the same or less money than he was getting in his last selling job. Face facts: he's an idiot, in trouble, or his present boss is a yahoo.
2 If you're looking for salesmen with experience, make sure you find out in detail *what* experience they've had. Just seven years on the road is no use at all. Remember the old joke about the army good-conduct medal – seven years of undetected crime. What you want to see are league tables, congratulatory memos from the boss, turnover graphs, commission statements, the salesman's own plan for how he covered his last territory, evidence of how he handled his reporting, his personal performance ratios and how these have steadily improved. He's also got to have a sound reason for wanting to leave his present company if he is successful. Beware of personality clashes with the boss – he may have one with you, too.

Any experienced salesman who cannot (or will not) produce such evidence has clearly not bothered collecting it, in which case he doesn't think right – and generally will be conning you into believing he's been successful when actually he's a failure.
3 Always, but always, take up references. And don't ever do it

by letter. Do it by telephone. No ex-boss is going to say anything nasty in writing about a past employee. But if you ask the right questions by telephone – open-ended questions (why? what? how? when? which? where? who?) – you'll get the answers that you're looking for.

4 Check even more thoroughly into work habits, motivation, how the prospective employee got on with his colleagues and superiors, if you are recruiting anyone *without* previous sales experience.

5 Before finally deciding, make up a foursome for dinner – you and your wife; he and his wife. Find out whether his wife is going to be an asset or a hindrance. If you've got two candidates who come pretty close, pick the one whose wife is going to back him up.

6 Beware unmarried salesmen. Often they get even more tired than married ones, their territory plans frequently resemble that old joke about the sailor's girl in every port, and their shelter/security motivation levels can be quite low. But there are lots of exceptions.

SALESMAN SELECTION CHART

Performance factors	Far exceeds job requirements	Exceeds job requirements	Meets job requirements	Needs some improvements	Does not meet requirements
QUALITY	Leaps tall buildings single bound.	Must take running start to leap over tall buildings.	Can only leap over a building with no spires.	Crashes into buildings when attempting to jump.	Cannot recognise buildings at all, much less jump
TIMELINESS	Is faster than a speeding bullet	Is as fast as a speeding bullet	Not as fast as a speeding bullet	Would you believe a slow bullet	Wounds self with bullets
INITIATIVE	Is stronger than a locomotive	Is stronger than a bull elephant	Is stronger than a bull	Shoots the bull	Smells like a bull
ADAPTABILITY	Walks on water consistently	Walks on water in emergencies	Washes with water	Drinks water	Passes water in emergencies
COMMUNICATION	Talks with God	Talks with the angels	Talks to himself	Argues with himself	Loses the arguments!

And don't forget . . .

When the new salesman starts work, give him a hero's welcome. Make him see that everyone thinks he is important. Get everyone properly briefed to make the new man's first few weeks as professional and as meaningful as they can be. Otherwise you'll probably demotivate him before he even starts selling for you.

Remuneration Schemes

Most salesmen perform better if they have an incentive. So do most sales managers.

A person's basic salary should be high enough to satisfy his own and his family's basic needs: mortgage, food, clothes, school fees, furniture, holidays, eating out occasionally, etc. If the salary doesn't achieve this, there could be problems – of a moonlighting nature, or worse. The salary should also be linked to the cost of living index – after all, the prices charged for the company's products or services are.

In addition to basic salary, the salesman and the manager should have some kind of commission on sales achieved.

Commission should *never* be paid on *all* sales achieved. Then it ceases to provide any incentive and becomes akin to the basic salary. Commission should start at a point on the sales turnover graph when the saleman's costs to the company have been covered – his breakeven point – or a little higher up the graph. Something like 75–80 per cent of sales target is reasonable.

Then, the rate of commission should *increase* progressively as sales turnover increases. Say 1 per cent from 80 per cent to target; 1½ per cent from target to 125 per cent; 2 per cent from 125 per cent to 150 per cent and (if the company can afford to lose the margin) 5 per cent for any sales over 150 per cent of target.

Targets, of course, have to be set properly, with the full involvement of the salesman, and be attainable. Read the sections on Forecasting and Setting Targets to find out how to achieve this.

Once properly set, targets, like territories, should be fixed, not adjusted annually. Thus the salesman can see his efforts earning him more and more money, and the company likewise makes more and more money. Only if the product range is changed should targets be interfered with once they have been set and proved workable.

Read the section on Growth if this concept gives you hysterics.

Profitability bonuses are a waste of time. Every salesman knows that the directors, the accountants and the auditors between them can make a laughing stock of the true profit situation – for good 'tax avoidance' reasons, of course. If you want to add to the salary plus commission package, try some regular prize incentives like holidays or colour TVs.

Paying Commission

To be really meaningful, commission should be calculated and paid on a monthly basis, not on an annual basis. This means that most companies will need to break their annual sales targets down into twelve individual monthly targets, allowing variations for seasonal demands if these apply.

The only snag with this system of monthly payments is that if the salesman has a few really good months in the first half of the year, and then his performance falls off during the second half, the company could wind up paying him too much commission. If the company takes the money back, by deducting it from the salesman's basic salary, this is bound to cause ill will. Thus, it is usual for only two-thirds of due commission to be paid on a monthly basis, the balance being cumulated to form a lump sum at the end of the year, and from which any overpayments can be deducted. This also provides for the company which pays commission when the orders are actually received being able to deduct commission paid on any orders which are subsequently cancelled.

Figure 23 shows a sample monthly commission statement. It caters for three product groups, two having the same commission rates but different breakeven or base points and targets,

Name .... Area .... Period .... to ....

Objectives per period	Group 1 Products	Group 2 Products	Total Gps 1 & 2	Group 3 Products	Total
(1) Base (2) Target					
Cum. to date					
(3) Base (4) Target					
Actual sales invoiced					
(5) For period (6) Cum. to date					

Commission earned — cumulative to date

(7) First   £ _____   (Max. line 4 minus 3)   at 1%   £ _____
(8) Next   £ _____   (Max. line 6 minus 4)   at 2%   £ _____

(9) Total sales   £ _____   To agree with line 6

(10) Less: already paid   _____

(11) Now due (if negative treat as nil)
(12) Add: Group 3 commission at ½% Line 5
(13) Other commissions   _____

(14) Total gross commission
     Payable on period — payroll   £ _____

(15) Advance herewith at ⅔ gross   £ _____

Figure 23. Example of a monthly sales commission statement.

the third for, say, consumable items. There are many companies selling to industry where this type of format will fit, the main products being capital plant and the rest being materials, tooling, consumables, for use with the capital plant.

What about the Sales Manager?

At the beginning of this section, I said that the manager as well as the salesman should be paid commission. I boggle at the number of British companies tht expect their sales managers to lead the team well when their basic salaries are a couple of thousand pounds less than quite a few of their own salesmen's salary plus commission.

The manager's salary should be significantly more than the salesmen's salaries. His commission element should be in the form of an overriding commission, again with a rate increasing as sales turnover increases. He may also be penalized for any of his salesmen not performing after a predetermined period of time.

Directors should be paid this way too. Then they'd stop moaning about paying their sales force far more than they are worth.

Sales Literature

I've tended to soft peddle on the subject of training in this book, although training is a most important and continual requirement in any sales force.

My main reason for soft peddling is because I believe a good sales manager (with a little help from his friends) can cover most of his ongoing training requirements through the use of car cassette programmes (see Utilizing Travelling Time) and through the company's sales literature.

Just like the car cassette concept and my thoughts on trade cycles, I have found very few companies willing to adopt the concept of training through the sales literature. But I shall keep trying.

Consider the fundamentals – you train because you want the salesmen to do the job in a certain way, and to think in a certain way.

The salesmen, being human after all, seek to do the job in the easiest way they can find. Most of their thinking is linked to this easiest way.

The easiest way for a salesman to conduct a sales presentation is to use his sales literature as the main framework of the presentation. He therefore uses the literature, the words in the literature, the pictures in the literature, the facts and figures in the literature.

The only snag is that the literature he uses wasn't designed to be his script for a sales presentation. It hardly ever contains anything about 'what's in it for the customer'. It rarely asks any questions. And it is never put together in the right order.

So most sales presentations which base themselves on the sales literature are something of a disaster.

Now wouldn't it be much more logical to design the sales literature to say what you want the salesman to say when he conducts his presentation? All it means is that you translate your sales training programme into words, pictures and pages in brochures.

Then you have a 'bible' which most of your salesmen will use automatically. In three months, they will know the *best method of presenting the products* off by heart. And you didn't spend a penny of your training budget – it all came out of the sales promotion budget.

Examples of 'bible' literature are very rare. Most of them are jobs I have done for companies over the past few years. It is impossible to illustrate them effectively in this book, so I'm afraid that if you want to learn more about how to design sales literature to sell you'll have to give me a ring at Structured Training Ltd.

Service Contracts

Everyone in selling – the salesman, the area manager, the sales manager, the sales director – should have a written service contract. Not just the bare minimum to satisfy the legal requirements of the Contracts of Employment Act and the Employment Protection Act, but a meaningful document which clearly defines what is what.

A properly designed service contract can do a lot to alleviate worry – that cancer which eats away at a person's performance in times when the going gets rough, when business is hard to get, when personalities clash. And you know it – there are plenty of those times.

A good service contract protects both employee and employer – and it should. Here is a sample contract, with appropriate notes, which could be tailored to fit practically everyone in the sales team, from salesman to director.

This agreement is made the ....day of.............. 19 .... between
.... whose registered office is at.........
.... (hereinafter called the company) of the one
part and .... of ....
(hereinafter called the employee) of the other part.

Whereby it is agreed as follows

The company hereby engages the services of the employee and
the employee accepts the engagement by the company as
.... upon the terms and conditions hereinafter
contained.

The employment shall begin on .... and shall continue until determined in accordance with the provisions hereinafter contained.

Duties

The employee shall under the direction of the board of directors
of the company (hereinafter called the board) be responsible for
and shall perform such duties and exercise such powers as from
time to time may be assigned to or vested in him in such capacity
by the board.

[*Authority comes from the board, although the employee may
report to a manager who is not a member of the board. Doing this
enables the original contract to stay in force without major revision
if the employee is subsequently promoted from salesman to sales
manager, or further. The details which* do *change are normally in-
cluded in separate conditions of employment and job description
which are referred to in the main service contract.*]

Attention to Duties

The employee unless prevented by ill health shall during the
term of his engagement devote the whole of his attention to the
business of the company. He shall not without the prior consent
in writing of the board be directly or indirectly concerned in any
other business during the term hereof.

Remuneration

The company shall pay to the employee a salary of £— per annum and such commission as his conditions of employment define. Such salary to be paid in equal monthly instalments in arrears on the last day of each month and such commission to be paid as defined in the conditions of employment.

The said salary shall not be less than £— per annum and shall be reviewed on the 1 January 19— and on the 1 January in each succeeding year in accordance with the changes in the cost of living as indicated by the general index of retail prices issued by the authority of Her Majesty's Government and published monthly by the Department of Employment (hereinafter called the index) and with the index figure (hereinafter called the basic figure) of the Index last published before the 1 January 19—.

On the 1 January 19— and on the 1 January of each succeeding year of the period of this agreement the said sum of £— shall be increased by the percentage thereof which corresponds to the percentage increase (if any) over the basic figure of the index figure last published before the said review takes place.

[*Note that the inclusion of such an 'inflation-proofing' clause may be deemed unenforceable if written during a time when it contravenes current government legislation. However, it does declare the company's intention, and, as such, is very reassuring to the employee.*]

Expenses

The company shall reimburse to the employee all reasonable travelling, hotel and other expenses properly incurred by him in the performance of his duties hereunder.

Provision of Company Car

The company shall provide the employee with a motorcar for his use and shall pay all expenses of maintaining, servicing and renewing the said motorcar including insurances and licences thereof and shall reimburse the employee the cost of all petrol and oil consumed while the said motorcar is used for business purposes during the course of the employment of the employee as hereunder.

[*It says nothing about private use, nor does it exclude private use. Thus, the company can make a separate ruling on this if it wishes.*]

Confidentiality

The employee shall not (except in the proper course of his duties as hereinunder) either during or after the period of his employment divulge to any person and shall use his best endeavours to prevent the publication or disclosure of any trade secret or manufacturing process or any information concerning the business or finances of the company or any of its dealings transactions or affairs which have come to his knowledge during the course of his employment.

Company Property

Any equipment, papers, documents, sales aids, samples, records and other articles supplied by the company to the employee remain the property of the company and must not be damaged or destroyed by the employee and on request by the company or if no longer required by the employee must be returned to the company.

[*Note that copies of any documents will be deemed by the courts to be the property of the owner of the original documents.*]

Restraint Clauses

The employee will not within the United Kingdom [*or wherever applicable*] and within two years after ceasing to be employed as hereinunder without the previous consent of the board in writing either alone or jointly with or as manager or agent for any person, firm or company directly or indirectly carry on or be engaged in the business of manufacturers and/or suppliers of ....

....

.... [*list company's products*.]. The employee will not within two years of ceasing to be employed as hereinunder either on his own behalf or on behalf of any person, firm or company directly or indirectly solicit, interfere with or endeavour to entice away from the company any employee or any person, firm or company who has at any time in the two years immediately preceding the determination of the employment of the employee done business with the company provided that nothing contained in this clause shall be deemed to prohibit the employee seeking or procuring orders or doing business with persons, firms or companies in connection with business not related or similar to the business of the company.

Inventions

The employee agrees that any invention, discovery, design or improvement made by him at any time during his employment with the company and in any way connected with or applicable to the products manufactured by and sold by or the methods of manufacture of such products by the company belongs to the company and that he will forthwith disclose the same to the company and that:

(i)   He will not without the written consent of the board apply for letters patent in the United Kingdom or in any other part of the world for any invention, discovery, design or improvement so made by him.

(ii)   He will if and whenever required so to do by the company apply as nominee of the company or join with it in applying for letters patent in the United Kingdom or in any other part of the world for any invention, discovery, design or improvement so made by him as the company shall in its sole discretion decide and will at all times sign all such documents and do all such things as may be requisite and desirable to vest the said letters patent when granted and all the right title and interest to and in the same in the company absolutely as sole beneficial owner or as the company may direct.

The company agrees to pay all expenses in connection with

such applications for letters patent made by the employee as nominee for or jointly with the company and will hold him indemnified against all liabilities in connection with or arising out of such application or letters patent when granted.

The term 'letters patent' in this agreement shall mean and include letters patent, *brevet d'invention*, petty patent, *gebrauchmuster*, utility model design registration or any other form of protection or improvement that can be obtained in the United Kingdom or in any other part of the world.

[*Every single employee of a company, from shop floor to directors, should agree to these 'inventions' clauses. It is the company's life blood at stake. I've seen far too many companies go bust because immoral employees have taken the best of the ideas, started up in competition, and stolen the market.*]

Holidays

The employee shall be entitled to such holidays with full pay as the company shall notify the employee are appropriate to the employee for the time being in accordance with the regulations of the company relating thereto notified from time to time to the staff of the company.

[*Details contained in the employee's conditions of employment or a more general staff notice.*]

Illness

The company shall pay the aforementioned salary in full whilst the employee shall be unable to fulfil his duties as hereinunder because of illness, physical or mental disability or other cause beyond his control up to a maximum period in the aggregate of 40 working days in any consecutive 52 week period. During any additional period of incapacity as aforesaid up to an additional period of 40 working days in any consecutive 52 week period such salary shall be reduced by one-half and thereafter until the employee shall have resumed his full duties he shall not be enentitled to any salary.

[*Often companies add a clause covering a reduction of salary in proportion to National Insurance payments received by employees whilst off sick, otherwise, some employees could earn more in their first 40 days whilst sick than whilst working.*]

Pension Scheme

The employee after completing the appropriate qualifying period shall join the company contributory superannuation scheme. The contribution level shall be that appropriate to his grade at the time of joining.

Termination of Employment

Except as hereinafter provided this agreement shall continue in force unless determined during the first six months by either party giving the other one full calendar month notice and thereafter three full calendar months notice in writing. The company shall be entitled to give payment in lieu of notice.

If the employee is at any time guilty of gross misconduct, neglect of his duties or refusal to carry out any order lawfully given to him by the company then the company shall be entitled to determine this agreement without notice or payment in lieu of notice.

The company shall be entitled to determine this agreement by notice in writing if the employee shall be convinced of an indicable offence other than an offence under the Road Traffic Acts provided that if the employee shall have lost his driving licence as a result of a conviction for an offence under the Road Traffic Acts and in the opinion of the board is unable to carry out his duties as hereinunder to the satisfaction of the board then the company may determine the employment of the employee in the manner provided in this clause.

Dress

The employee shall during the continuance of this agreement observe the requirements of the company as to the style of dress and general appearance expected of a representative of the company and failure to so comply shall be grounds for determination as aforesaid.

Conclusion

As witness the hand of .... on behalf of
.... and the hand of the employee the day
and year first above written.

Signed by

On behalf of

In the presence of

Signed by

In the presence of

[*Note that two copies of the agreement should be signed, both in
the presence of witnesses – one copy for the company, one for the
employee. But don't put it all together yourself. Get the company's
solicitors to do the final draft.*]

Conditions of Employment

Whether there is a properly drafted service agreement or not,
every employer is required by law to give every employee the
following information in writing. Items already covered in a
service agreement may be omitted; the rest forming the conditions of employment document already referred to.

1 Name and address of employer and employee.
2 Date employment commences. (If previous service with
  another employer is regarded as part of the employment, as
  in a takeover situation or a transfer within a group, the *earliest*
  date of commencement is applicable.)
3 Salary level and methods of calculating all types of remuneration relevant.
4 Intervals at which payments are made.
5 Hours of work and any terms and conditions that apply.
6 Holiday entitlements, including statutory.
7 Terms and conditions relating to sickness or injury, including payment provisions.

8 Pension scheme details, including details of 'contracting out' certificate if relevant.
9 Notice of termination periods.
10 Job title.
11 Specific disciplinary rules, other than those relating to health and safety.
12 Name of person to whom the employee should apply if dissatisfied with any disciplinary action taken against him.
13 Name and position of person to whom the employee can apply if seeking redress for any grievance relating to his employment.

Strengths and Weaknesses

You need to know your own, your company's, your competitors', your salesmen's, your market's, your management team's strengths and weaknesses.

Make a list of all of them, a kind of 'pro' and 'con' list. And don't ever kid yourself.

Use the lists as the basis for your strategic and tactical planning, your training programmes, your sales promotion plans and for product development.

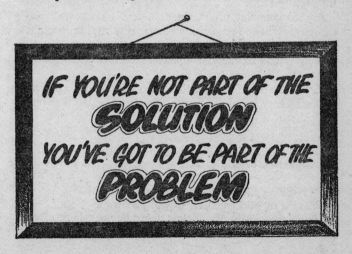

Supplier Evaluation

Is your company prepared and willing to submit itself to a supplier evaluation and assessment? Have any of your present customers ever conducted one on you, or suggested the idea? As you expand your markets into the future, will you be ready for it when it happens?

Supplier evaluation is a purchasing technique being introduced by more and more buying departments of large organizations. What the customers are trying to establish, in quantifiable terms, is their supplier's total capability to supply their requirements – at the right time, at the right quality and at the right price.

The forward-looking sales manager can prepare his company and his salesmen to meet the requirements of any such evaluation or assessment. This preparation usually takes the form of a specially designed piece of sales literature called a company profile. Build such a profile into your budget, and you will not only put your company at the top of the league table in the professional buyer's estimation, you will provide your salesmen with most of the ammunition and knowledge they need to master the commercial and financial aspects of their selling tasks.

A good company profile contains details of the company's capacity, plant and production equipment, inspection and test facilities, range of customers, future plans, ownership, key executives and labour and financial record over the past five years.

Here are a list of some of the questions to which a potential customer may require answers when conducting a supplier evaluation:

Technical Aspects

1 Has the supplier an adequate design staff?
2 Has the supplier an effective quality control?
3 Is the technical staff sufficient to handle the volume of work we require plus the supplier's other commitments?

4 Are the test and inspection facilities and equipment adequate to meet our standards?
5 Are the facilities for handling rejects and repairs satisfactory?
6 Is the production plant and machinery good enough, reliable enough and accurate enough to meet our standards?
7 Is there sufficient skilled manpower?
8 Is there adequate technical representation and liaison should the need arise?
9 Is the instruction and training facility adequate?
10 Is the supplier capable of interpreting our drawings and specifications?

Commercial Aspects

1 Are the supplier's financial resources adequate?
2 Is the management structure effective?
3 What is the supplier's delivery record?
4 How reliable and stable are the prices?
5 What are the supplier's relations with its own workforce like? Is the supplier strike-prone?
6 Has the supplier room for expansion if the need arose?
7 Is there adequate labour in the area?
8 Are the supplier's executives and customer liaison people easy to communicate with?
9 Is the supplier easy to reach from our headquarters?

10 Has the supplier a reliable and professional purchasing and supply department and system within itself?
11 Does the supplier carry adequate stocks?
12 Is the guarantee satisfactory?
13 Has the supplier a competent accounts system that will deal quickly and simply with any invoice or account query?
14 Is the supplier's policy and procedure for rejects and returns satisfactory?
15 Has the supplier adequate transport?
16 Is the sales force competent and available quickly?

Questions for Overseas Agents and Importers

1 Has the agent adequate technical knowledge of his principal's products?
2 Can the agent give the necessary technical back-up and advice?
3 Is the agent competent with his import procedures?
4 What are his relations with his principals?
5 Is he financially sound?

Third-Party References

And after you have answered all these questions, the potential customer is more than likely going to finish up by asking you for the names of at least three of your regular established customers that he can contact and find out what they *really* think of you as a supplier. So have some good third-party references already primed and available.

Traitor

I spend a fair proportion of my consultancy time sorting out purchasing departments as well as sales departments. Let's face it, shouldn't supply and demand be as close together as possible?

Here is a list of questions I suggest buyers should ask the many, many salesmen who persist in wasting their time rather than getting down to business. You may care to pass this list to your own salesmen and tell them to be sure they have the answers for every call they make. One day, they are sure to come across a buyer who has spent some time with Fenton.

1 Why did you take the trouble to come and see me ?
2 Why do you feel your products will be of benefit to us ?
3 Why do you feel your product is better for us than the one we are using ?
4 What will we gain by using/selling this ?
5 Please, your time as well as my time is very expensive. Can you get to the point ?

Team Spirit

Don't ever let your salesmen feel they are in competition with one another. If they do, they'll hold back vital information which could be of benefit to everyone.

Every time you get the sales force together, devote at least half an hour to an information tank. Get the team working as a team. Pick one thorny general objection to each meeting, and get everyone contributing to find the best way of dealing with that objection. Then make sure each and every one of your salesmen can *use* that best way. Do this consistently for a few months and everyone will get the message.

It's teamwork that gets the best results.

Territories and Targets

Once you have got them right, don't ever change the salesmen's territories. This will demotivate like nothing else.

Only if a salesman leaves can you afford to review the territory situation, and then only very carefully.

Likewise, if you have set targets linked to commission earnings, those targets, once set, should remain the same. That is not to say that your *sales turnover* targets should be frozen – only the *base* targets from which commission payments begin.

In other words, if a salesman develops his territory over a number of years, he should be rewarded progressively for all his efforts in this development, not chopped back each year

THESE SALESMEN FAILED TO MAKE TARGET

and be made to start all over again for the same amount of commission earnings. Don't be greedy, or you will lose your best men.

Only in the event of price increases should commission-related base targets be amended. Everyone will see this as fair. It's really the number of orders that count.

Titles

Don't use titles indiscriminately. Don't make a salesman an area manager unless he's got at least one salesman to manage. Don't ever use titles to motivate a salesman. You'll upset your company's management structure and it will be hell's own delight getting it right again.

Have a sliding scale of sizes of company car and use this instead. You'll find it much more effective and it gives you only *one* problem – overcoming the internal politics of giving a senior salesman a bigger car than the company secretary runs. Don't laugh, this is true for most of British industry.

Trade Cycles

Don't let them fool you. Don't even believe them.

I've lost count of the number of times I've helped a company's products take off like a rocket when all their competitors in the market were going downhill fast in accordance with the known trade cycle. Here's an example.

In 1974 we introduced a brand new machine – a Russian machine – on to the British market at a time when the trade cycle for home market machine tool sales was descending at 30 per cent to the vertical. With a new approach to the techniques of selling machine tools, based on finance, not on product features, a one-day training course on how to demonstrate the new machines, a press conference and press demonstration, and some likewise different advertising over a three-month period, the importing company increased its home market share from 2 per cent to 50 per cent in one year. Total cost of devising the marketing plan, training the sales force, designing the literature and adverts and handling press relations – £6,500.

All it needed was a bit of original salesmanship and some enthusiasm. Everyone else was just sitting back and kidding themselves that there was no point trying to sell that year, because the trade cycle said it wasn't possible.

If you *really* want a dilly of an example of how a whole industry has kidded itself for more than twenty years, it has to be our beloved British machine tool industry. All the major manufacturers in this industry advocate limiting major machine tool trade exhibitions in Britain to once every four years. They say they cannot afford more frequent exhibitions.

So what have exhibitions got to do with trade cycles and people kidding themselves, you may be saying? Well, consider the graph in figure 24. It depicts net home market machine tool orders since 1957 adjusted to take out all price increases.

Pinpointed on this graph, you see the times Britain held its major international machine tool shows. Coincidence do you think, that the date of the show always coincides with a peak in the trade cycle?

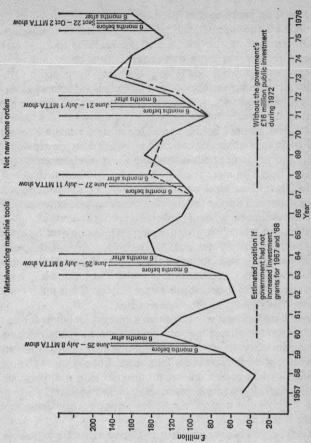

Figure 24. Graph showing new orders of metalworking machine tools in the UK home market from 1957 to 1976.

No. The peaks in this particular trade cycle have to be caused by the international machine tool shows themselves. Consider how all the salesmen in the machine tool industry would react to the news that in six months time, they again spend ten days whooping it up at Olympia or the NEC. Consider all the new sales literature, new models, additional advertising, press releases, invitations to customers etc., going out during the six-month build-up to each show. Consider how all this activity would bolster the enthusiasm of practically every salesman in the machine tool business – and how easy it would be to convert some of this enthusiasm into extra business.

And in the six months after each show, consider how long it would take these same salesmen to follow up all the inquiries they generated during the shows themselves, and how many of these inquiries they would convert into orders.

It's just a whole industry jumping up and down at the same time – extra activity and enthusiasm equals a rising trade cycle.

If you really want to wonder what's going on in this country – match my graph with the national trade cycle for Britain and with the trade cycle for Western Europe. Then tell me it's just a coincidence that they look so alike.

Machine tools are one of Britain's general economic indicators. Everything else tends to follow the trend set by machine tools. So ask yourself why the machine tool industry is still advocating exhibitions every four years, when it could change Britain's trade cycle from say a four-year loop to a two-year loop, simply by having its major show every two years.

I suppose it's a chicken and egg situation, but doesn't it make you sick?

Okay, if you believe only half of all that, what are you going to do to thumb your nose at your own trade cycle? Because, if it's true for machine tools, it's true for every other industry.

All you've got to do is sell it to them!

Training Salesmen

Training is the key factor of personal development, and without personal development your salesmen will quickly get fed up and leave for pastures new.

The development of a salesman need not necessarily be towards promotion to management. Many managers never realize this. A salesman can be developed so that he remains happy being a salesman, yet his abilities and his knowledge are regularly updated, so that his value to the company is continually increasing, and he can see that this is so.

There are at least eight different areas of the selling job where regular and continuous training is essential:

1 Product knowledge.
2 Application knowledge.
3 Competitors' products and applications.
4 Customers' businesses and their trends.
5 Customers' markets and their trends.
6 Selling techniques.
7 Planning techniques.
8 Commercial and financial knowledge.

If you do some of this training yourself, make sure your presentation is as professional as if you were negotiating the biggest order of your life. Prepare everything, lay out the meeting room properly, ban all interruptions, use professionally produced visual aids, lay on refreshments, and above all get the objectives clear and make the whole proceedings look to everyone there as if they are critically important – which, damn it, they are.

Unwinding

How do you unwind after a hard day at the office, or out in the field?

Stereo? Scotch? Squash? Sex?

You need something. I've got a Ludwig drum kit permanently set up in my den, with eighty watts of quadraphonic to back it up. Ten minutes beating hell out of that to Ted Heath and I'm a new man.

People who cannot unwind get very tired very fast. Find a way that fits you, and find it fast.

USP

Whatever happened to USP?

In the days before marketing clouded everyone's thoughts on what selling and sales management were all about, USP was a critical part of the manager's training armoury.

It stands for *unique selling point*.

Every product has at least one, otherwise no one would ever buy the product. USP is the 'edge' your product has over its competitors. USP is the difference which makes customers buy yours rather than someone else's or something else.

Find out what the USP is for every one of your products or services. And once you know, don't lose sight of the fact that, if you are up against strong competition, USP is all you've got to sell.

Utilizing Travelling Time

I've got a hobby horse.

I've had it for several years. It frustrates me, it infuriates me. I cannot understand why someone somewhere doesn't do something about it. I've tried many times to interest sales managers and directors in the concept, but I've never once succeeded. So maybe it's a lousy concept. I don't think so, and I'll never have a better opportunity of shouting about it, so here goes . . .

More than 40 per cent of a salesman's total time is spent in his car, travelling from A to B and back again. Apart from a little thinking from time to time, about what happened on the last call and what is likely to happen on the next, this 40 per cent of total time is pretty useless for the salesman – and for his company.

So how about using it for ongoing product training, application training and for disseminating information about the competition, the markets, changes in company policies, *and* for those frequent inspirational messages from the boss ?

All you need to do is equip each salesman's car with a cassette player and provide him, through the post, with the necessary cassette tapes. Ten minutes maximum of business on each tape, laced with some good music and even finishing with some key questions each salesman has to answer, just to make sure he plays the tape.

The initial investment on equipment would be amortized against just one day's meeting at HQ of the whole sales force.

Producing the tapes is easy. You could do it at home, or get a couple of members of the local operatic society to do the voices. Scripting is no more difficult than preparing a proposal or a new piece of sales literature. Alternatively, our training and consultancy company, Structured Training Ltd, would be delighted to do the job for you.

Selling Techniques

And if the concept works for you on product training, why not try it on salesmanship? How's this for a list of ten-minute cassettes – cassettes which the salesman can select and play while he is on his way to an important call...

Tape 1 What's the objective of your next call? How can you best start the interview?

Tape 2 You're going to conduct a detailed survey. What do you need, what do you look for, what questions do you need to ask the prospect?

Tape 3 You're taking a prospect to a demonstration. What does the prospect really need to see, what could go wrong, and why?

Tape 4 You're following up the quotation. How do you get him to say yes? What objections might you have to deal with? Do you know the best answers?

Tape 5 How can you persuade the prospect to give us a chance? He's been dealing with our competitors for so long, how best can you find out his criteria for ordering and match it to our products?

Tape 6 Is your offer cost-effective? Have you taken the trouble to find out how much the customer is going to make, or save, if he buys our product? And have you told him in a way which will enable him to convince his own directors?

Tape 7 What's in it for the customer? You know all the main features of our products – how does the customer benefit from these features – and how do you tell him?

Tape 8 Prospecting. What companies are most likely to buy our products – and why? Just exactly what are we selling – what is our 'edge'?

Tape 9 Getting more appointments – and at the best times. Dealing with the inquiries generated by our advertising.

Tape 10 Territory planning. What are you doing sitting in that car for 40 per cent of the day, when with a little attention to the routes you take you could spend at least 10 per cent of the wasted time selling to someone else.

And for the way home...

Tape 11 You lost the order. Why? Can you make sure you never make the same mistakes again?

Just as a bonus, here are a couple of tapes for the sales manager who, of course, needs to be fully conversant with all eleven . . .

Tape 12 Training salesmen on the job. What to do with that one day a month out there in the field with each man.
Tape 13 Counselling. You have a salesman with a problem. What do you do about it – and how?

That's my hobby horse, then. Any takers?

V

Visual Aids

Give your salesmen some kind of effective visual aids which they can use to back up their verbal presentations, preferably something the customers can get their hot sticky hands on. The literature is never enough.

If you are selling fasteners, make sure all your salesmen carry, and use, the widest selection of samples. If you are selling castings, likewise, cut-away to show the texture and uniformity of grain if this is important.

If you sell switchgear, electronic components, instrumentation, controls, anything small and intricate, make sure your

Figure 25.

salesmen have plenty of bits and pieces for the customers to play with.

Samples of this kind are critical.

The UK's largest vending machine company, GKN-Sankey, introduced a new model in 1977 with a unique digital drink selection panel, like a giant pocket calculator. Each salesman was provided with a panel, straight out of production, which he could use to demonstrate to a customer how the new digital system worked (figure 25). The customers and the salesmen were delighted, both with the sample panel, complete with special carrying case, and with how easy it made explaining and understanding the new machine.

W

Why Not, Why Not?

I've pinched this from Sir Barnes Wallis, the aircraft designer responsible for those fantastic bouncing bombs used by the Dam Busters in the Second World War, blockbuster 'earthquake' bombs and a host of other way-out but highly successful devices. It's his favourite expression.

Sir Barnes Wallis never conformed to traditional ways of doing a job. He looked for, and found, the different approach. A good sales manager should think this way. Always on the lookout for a better way of selling, or presenting a product, or designing an advertisement, or packaging or exhibiting.

It is the *gimmick* that whets the appetite of the customer these days. As long as it is a good gimmick. So to hell with the conventions and the traditional ways of doing the job. Be original – and be more successful.

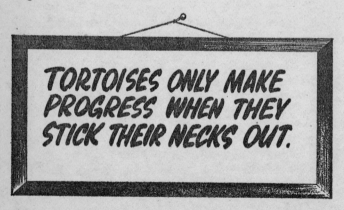

TORTOISES ONLY MAKE PROGRESS WHEN THEY STICK THEIR NECKS OUT.

Xmas Presents

The only kind of Christmas present worth giving a customer is one that will stay in his place of business for a long time (at least until *next Christmas*), reminding him every day that you are one of his most reliable and loyal suppliers.

Cases of whisky, once drunk, are soon forgotten. Presents that the customer takes home to his wife are likewise out of sight and out of mind.

So don't ever lose sight of the fact that Christmas presents are part of your *sales promotion* budget. Give presents that *are* strictly sales promotion, and you maximize the return on the investment as well as avoiding all smells of bribery and corruption.

The list of things you can give customers at Christmas time is endless. Prices, too, can range from a few pence to a few hundred pounds. Whatever you choose, always make sure your company name, address and telephone number is on the gift and always bear in mind that the gift *must* reflect the corporate identity of your company.

What I mean by that is – if you sell cheap and cheerful products, you can bestow a cheap and cheerful gift. If you sell the best and most expensive products, your gifts need to match this.

A word on girlie calendars. This is a highly competitive field, and not all your customers may care to display your calendar in their offices. Yours has to be better and classier than Pirelli in its heyday. If you can't afford the quality, forget girls.

The Ultimate

The perfect business gift, the ultimate, used to sit on my office desk, black and slightly sinister, bearing the name, address and telephone number of the firm that gave it to me (figure 26).

A slot in its top took a 5p piece. The coin rested in the slot, making an electrical contact which caused the whole box to vibrate, heave about and emit a gravelly graveyard-style grinding noise. A trapdoor in the top then slowly opened, a horrible green slimy hand crept out, gently took hold of the 5p coin and then – faster than the eye could follow – hand and coin were gone, trapdoor was closed tight and the black box was still and silent.

You had to witness it really to appreciate the artistry of the mechanism.

So consider the factors that made this black box the ultimate business gift. It sits on a customer's desk, making him money. Every time someone tries it, he makes 5p. Your competitor visits him, sees your name on the box and says, 'What's all this then?' Customer smiles and replies, 'Cost you 5p to find out.' (Have you ever taken money off the competition before?)

Figure 26. A 'black box' — the ultimate business gift.

If the box goes wrong, the customer loses his income from it, and the pleasure he gets from showing people the thing. So he telephones you.

Certainly you can replace it. Oh, by the way, what is happening with that job we quoted for last month?

Yahoo

If you don't know what it means, look it up in a dictionary.

You will be well on the way to being one when your staff start hanging notices like this all round the office:

> WE THE WILLING, LED BY THE UNKNOWN,
> ARE ACHIEVING THE IMPOSSIBLE FOR
> THE UNGRATEFUL.
>
> WE HAVE DONE SO MUCH FOR SO LONG
> WITH SO LITTLE, WE ARE NOW QUALIFIED
> TO DO ANYTHING WITH NOTHING.

Z

Zest

Don't ever let the zest go out of the job. Don't let the brass get you down or the job start running you. If you do, you might as well give up and start growing mushrooms.

Always let your salesmen see your best side. Keep that wet Thursday in Workington feeling for when you get home. I know it's not fair on the wife, but she'll understand; your salesmen won't.

Your job satisfaction is just as important as your salesmen's. I hope this book will help you put a little more zest into your job and provide you with a few tips that will help you increase your job satisfaction, your results and your take-home pay. If it does, please drop me a line at Structured Training Ltd or the Institute of Sales Management and let me know. It could help *my* job satisfaction.

Postscript

The Indispensable Man

Sometime, when you're feeling important,
Sometime, when your ego's in bloom,
Sometime, when you take it for granted
You're the best informed man in the room,

Take a bucket and fill it with water,
Put your hand in it up to the wrist,
Pull it out and the hole that remains there
Is the measure of how you'll be missed.

You may splash all you please as you enter,
You may stir up the water galore
But stop! and you'll see in a moment
That it looks just the same as before.

The moral of this simple story
Is do just the best that you can,
'Cause you'll find that in spite of vainglory
There is no 'indispensable man'.

Source unkown

MEMO REF:

THE CURRENT CRISIS

In view of the current financial crisis the following figures
may be of interest:

Population of Country	54,000,000
People aged 65 and over	14,000,000
Balance left to do the work	40,000,000
People aged 18 and under	18,000,000
Balance left to do the work	22,000,000
Union members	9,000,000
Balance left to do the work	13,000,000
People in Armed Forces	2,300,000
Balance left to do the work	10,700,000
Government, local government and other civil servants	9,800,000
Balance left to do the work	900,000
People who won't work	888,000
Balance left to do the work	12,000
People in prison	11,998
Balance left to do the work	2

You and I, therefore, must work harder, particularly you,
as I am really fed up with running this joint on my own.

John Fenton
How to Double Your Profits
Within the Year £1.50

A programme of improvements, applicable to all types of business, to help you at least double your profits within twelve months. Fictional but highly practical, the book is an extended memorandum, an action plan, written by the MD of an imaginary company to his top managers. It shows, for example, how you can choose which customers contribute most to your profitability; recruit the right people; improve production efficiency; price for maximum profit; control your sales force. In the few hours it takes to read the book, you will be convinced that the title's claim is a modest understatement.

R. E. Palmer and A. H. Taylor
Financial Planning and Control £1.75

Today, more than ever before, it is essential that management has a sound appreciation of the financial implications of its plans and actions. Using clear, everyday language the authors explain the nature of the assistance which higher levels of accounting can provide in the planning and control of a modern business.

'It really is excellent value and offers an intensely practical approach' CERTIFIED ACCOUNTANTS JOURNAL

C. Northcote Parkinson and Nigel Rowe
Communicate £1.20

Parkinson's formula for business survival

Peter Drucker says in his Foreword: 'This book, to my knowledge for the first time, tackles all four elements of communication (what to say; when to say it; whom to say it to; how to say it). It makes the businessman literate and it gives him the competence which he needs.'

'Will be read avidly by the professionals and the amateurs in PR, but it is the individual businessman who will gain most from it' DIRECTOR

Peter F. Drucker
Management £2.50

Peter Drucker's aim in this major book is 'to prepare today's and tomorrow's managers for performance'. He presents his philosophy of management, refined as a craft with specific skills: decision making, communication, control and measurement, analysis – skills essential for effective and responsible management in the late twentieth century.

'Crisp, often arresting . . . A host of stories and case histories from Sears Roebuck, Marks and Spencer, IBM, Siemens, Mitsubishi and other modern giants lend colour and credibility to the points he makes' ECONOMIST

Managing for Results 95p

'A guide to do-it-yourself management . . . contains first-class suggestions that have the great virtue that they are likely to be widely and easily applicable to almost every business' TIMES REVIEW OF INDUSTRY

'Excellent . . . well-supported examples of what has happened in practice to companies that have thought in this analytical way' FINANCIAL TIMES

The Practice of Management £1.95

'Peter Drucker has three outstanding gifts as a writer on business – acute perception, brilliant skill as a reporter and unlimited self-confidence . . . his penetrating accounts of the Ford Company . . . Sears Roebuck . . . IBM . . . are worth a library of formal business histories' NEW STATESMAN

'Those who now manage ought to read it: those who try to teach management ought to buy it' TIMES EDUCATIONAL SUPPLEMENT

Peter F. Drucker
The Effective Executive £1.25

'A specific and practical book about how to be an executive who
contributes . . . The purpose of this book is to induce the executive
to concentrate on his own contribution and performance, with his
attention directed to improving the organization by serving
outsiders better. I believe Mr Drucker achieves this purpose
simply and brilliantly — and in the course of doing so offers many
insights into executive work and suggestions for improving
executive performance. I can conscientiously recommend that this
book be given the very highest priority for executive reading and
even rereading' DIRECTOR

Rosemary Stewart
The Reality of Organizations £1.25

'Addressed to managers whether in industry, commerce, hospitals,
public administration or elsewhere and includes examples from
these latter fields . . . its style is excellent, concise and free of
jargon' PUBLIC ADMINISTRATION

The Reality of Management £1.25

'Not just another manual for executives, it is rather more like a set
of compass bearings to help the manager plot his course in his
career and his social life' NEW SOCIETY

Alastair Mant
The Rise and Fall of the British Manager
£1.20

'Seeks to explain, in a vigorous style, why in this country we
"downgrade so many of the jobs that really matter . . ." Mant
argues that the business of making and selling things, and doing
these jobs well, has been submerged by the preoccupation with
"management", as if it was something quite distinct from these
humdrum activities' FINANCIAL TIMES

'What ails the British economy, he claims, is not the quality of its
management, but the fact that management exists at all'
NEW STATESMAN

'Managers and management teachers who are anxious to explore
new and more effective means of improving management
performance will not be deterred'
MANAGEMENT REVIEW AND DIGEST

Robert Taylor
The Fifth Estate £1.95

Are Britain's unions too weak or too powerful? Robber barons or
failed agents of social justice? Are they responsible for Britain's
postwar economic decline, or a constructive force?

Labour correspondent of the *Observer*, Robert Taylor examines
such questions, giving a highly readable profile of the trade union
movement, its history and structure. Revised and updated to the
May 1979 General Election, this will become the classic analysis
of the British unions in the late twentieth century.

'Invaluable . . . entertaining, informative and accurate'
ECONOMIST

'Essential reading' SCOTSMAN

Desmond Goch
Finance and Accounts for Managers £1.25

The art of accountancy is now the most important instrument of
control in the management armoury. This comprehensive guide
will enable managers — even those without formal training in
business finance — to formulate trading policies, forecast future
trends and effectively administer their departments.

Charles Handy
Gods of Management £1.25

What sort of manager are you — and what sort of manager is your
boss? Witty, imaginative, controversial and studded with real-life
management case histories, *Gods of Management* has the answer.

'The gods of management are engaged in a great battle, the out-
come of which could decide the future success of our
nation . . . Zeus, the dynamic entrepreneur . . . Apollo, the god
of order and bureaucracy . . . A man with a lifetime's experience,
Professor Handy has written one of the more stimulating books on
management' FINANCIAL TIMES

Margaret Hennig and Anne Jardim
The Managerial Woman £1.20

'Practical suggestions for women who are setting out on the
climb to the top' FINANCIAL TIMES

'Why do so many women founder on the lowly rungs of the
executive ladder? *The Managerial Woman* attempts to provide an
answer by telling ambitious women how to overcome the worst
pitfalls' DAILY MAIL

'For this book 3,000 women were involved in seminars or
interviews and twenty-five who had made it were interviewed in
great depth' DIRECTOR

Reference, Language and Information

☐ Passing Examinations	C. Allen	50p
☐ The Story of Language	C. L. Barber	95p
☐ North–South	Brandt Commission	£1.95p
☐ Trachtenberg Speed System of Basic Mathematics	A. Cutler and R. McShane	£1.25p
☐ One-Parent Families	Diana Davenport	85p
☐ Dictionary of Management	D. French and H. Saward	£1.50p
☐ Mathematics for the Million	L. Hogben	£1.95p
☐ Dictionary of Quotations	Robin Hyman	£1.25p
☐ Militant Islam	Godfrey Jansen	£1.25p
☐ Practical Statistics	R. Langley	£1.95p
☐ A Guide to Speaking in Public	Robert Seton Lawrence	85p
☐ How to Study	H. Maddox	£1.50p
☐ Dictionary of Life Sciences	E. A. Martin	£1.95p
☐ Getting the Right Job	Parsons and Neustatter	80p
☐ The Collector's Encyclopedia of Antiques	Phoebe Phillips	£2.95p
☐ The Modern Crossword Dictionary	Norman Pulsford	£1.75p
☐ Understanding Poetry	James Reeves	90p
☐ English Proverbs Explained		80p
☐ Pan Spelling Dictionary	Ronald Ridout	£1.50p
☐ Guide to Saving and Investment	James Rowlatt	£1.50p
☐ Names for Boys and Girls	L. Sleigh and C. Johnson	£1.25p
☐ Straight and Crooked Thinking	R. H. Thouless	£1.00p
☐ The Best English	G. H. Vallins	80p
☐ Better English		80p
☐ Biographical Encyclopedia of Science and Technology		£2.50p
☐ Cassell's Compact French-English, English-French Dictionary		£2.95p
☐ Cassell's Compact German-English, English-German Dictionary		£1.75p
☐ Cassell's Compact Spanish-English, English-Spanish Dictionary		£1.50p

Management

☐ **Biographical Encyclopedia of Science and Technology**	Isaac Asimov	£2.50p
☐ **The Effective Executive**	⎫	£1.25p
☐ **Management**	⎬ Peter Drucker	£2.50p
☐ **Managing for Results**	⎪	95p
☐ **Practice of Management**	⎭	£1.95p
☐ **Dictionary of Management**	D. French and H. Saward	£1.50p
☐ **Gods of Management**	Charles Handy	£1.25p
☐ **The Managerial Woman**	M. Hennig and A. Jardim	£1.20p
☐ **Practical Statistics**	R. Langley	£1.95p
☐ **A Guide to Speaking in Public**	Robert Seton Lawrence	85p
☐ **The Rise and Fall of the British Manager**	Alistair Mant	£1.20p
☐ **Communicate**	C. Northcote Parkinson	£1.20p
☐ **Guide to Saving and Investment**	James Rowlatt	£1.50p
☐ **Reality of Management**	⎫ Rosemary Stewart	£1.25p
☐ **Reality of Organisations**	⎭	£1.25p
☐ **Financial Planning for Managers**	A. H. Taylor and R. E. Palmer	£1.75p
☐ **Dictionary of Economics and Commerce**		£1.50p
☐ **Everyman's Roget's Thesaurus**		£1.95p
☐ **Multilingual Commercial Dictionary**		£1.95p

All these books are available at your local bookshop or newsagent, or can be ordered direct from the publisher. Indicate the number of copies required and fill in the form below

Name————————————————————————
(block letters please)

Address ————————————————————————

————————————————————————————————

Send to Pan Books (CS Department), Cavaye Place, London SW10 9PG
Please enclose remittance to the value of the cover price plus:

25p for the first book plus 10p per copy for each additional book ordered
to a maximum charge of £1.05 to cover postage and packing
Applicable only in the UK

While every effort is made to keep prices low, it is sometimes
necessary to increase prices at short notice. Pan Books reserve
the right to show on covers and charge new retail prices which
may differ from those advertised in the text or elsewhere